TIE-AND-DYE AS A PRESENT-DAY CRAFT

DEDICATED

TO

MY DEAR MOTHER AND FATHER

TIE-AND-DYE
as a
PRESENT-DAY CRAFT

by
ANNE MAILE

TAPLINGER PUBLISHING COMPANY
NEW YORK

MILLS & BOON LIMITED
London

First published 1963

Published in the United States by
TAPLINGER PUBLISHING CO., INC.
29 East Tenth Street
New York, New York, 10003

Published in London by MILLS AND BOON LIMITED

© Anne Maile 1963

2nd (revised) impression 1965

3rd impression 1967

4th (revised) printing 1969

New material in this edition © Anne Maile 1969

American SBN 8008-7700-4

British SBN 0000-0000-0

Library of Congress Catalog Number 76-107018

Printed in Great Britain

CONTENTS

Equipment
Wax and flour-paste
Protection for the hands
Templets

Marbling
Twisting and coiling

A length
A square
A triangle
An all-over pattern

Fastening-off methods
Untying
A slip knot
Dyed binding threads
Types of binding
Patterns made with binding:
    stripes
    circles
    spots
    clump tying

*   *   *   *

LIST OF PLATES

ACKNOWLEDGMENTS

I AM very grateful to the Principal, Mr. L. J. Daniels, A.R.C.A., Vice-Principal Mr. G. N. Monk, A.R.C.A. and Staff of the Textile Department at the Camberwell School of Arts and Crafts for their helpful co-operation over many years.

In particular I wish to thank Miss Karin Warming who has been my main source of inspiration. Right from the earliest clumsy experiments she has guided and encouraged me, always stimulating me to further efforts. Without her backing I should never have made any progress in the craft of tie-and-dye.

I appreciate the interest Mr. T. J. Corbin, A.R.C.A., has always shown in my work and the way he has championed tie-and-dye as a worth-while craft.

I should like to thank Mr. Rodney Moorhouse, B.Sc., DES.R.C.A., who has given me much valuable information on dyes.

To I.C.I., Ciba Clayton Ltd., Dylon International Ltd. and Bayer Dyestuffs Ltd. I am greatly indebted for the use of their dyestuffs.

CIBA of Basle, Switzerland, have kindly given me permission to use some of the historical facts from their CIBA Review No.104, "Plangi Tie-and-Dye Work" by A. Bühler.

The excellent black and white photographs were taken by Mr. Donald Smith, the frontispiece photograph by Basil Barnes Studios, London, and the other colour pictures by Messrs. Hydes and Speirs.

A. M.

PREFACE

WITH more and more people becoming interested in tie-and-dye, the lack of a practical instruction book on the subject has become apparent. It is hoped that this book will provide sufficient information to help all would-be " tie-dyers " and make them aware of the many possibilities of this fascinating craft.

The methods recommended here are not meant to be hard and fast rules, but rather to act as a guide, supplying a nucleus of suggestions for future experiments. Over many years I have accumulated a certain amount of " know-how " on ways of producing dyed and resist-dyed patterns on fabric. The instructions given are these common-sense methods, and do not claim to be authentic descriptions of traditional techniques. In fact, any knowledge of these is very limited.

In the past, men and women of many nationalities have found tie-dyeing a means of expressing their love of colour and pattern. Today, with the added advantage of our modern dyes, it is a very rewarding craft, for both sexes. Most people will be able to manage the majority of methods that require sewing. This need not be elaborate. Medium to large stitches sewn with a fair-sized needle will be adequate. The ability to pull up the thread tightly and fasten off securely to produce a definite resist is far more important.

Owing to the small amount of equipment needed, this craft can be carried out in the classroom and in the home. Some of the simpler methods are within the capabilities of the younger school child. The art or textile student can learn a great deal from becoming acquainted with this traditional form of fabric decoration, whilst the designer has an untapped source of patterns, textures and effects at his disposal. The dyed fabrics can be used for dresses, skirts, blouses, scarves, etc., and for many household articles.

Anyone wishing to see some Indian bandhana work would find an interesting selection at the Victoria and Albert Museum.

9

In the Ethnographical Section of the British Museum there are some typical examples of African work, whilst the Commonwealth Institute and the Horniman Museum have both African and Indian samples. There are at the time of writing (autumn 1965) plans to start a centre at the Horniman Museum where tie-dyed fabrics from many countries may be studied. The Museum's library already includes a number of books with historical references to the craft.

I can thoroughly recommend tie-and-dye, or " tie-dyeing " as a practical and satisfactory craft. There are the easy methods, giving quick results, besides those requiring more time and skill. But, simple or complicated, tie-and-dye fabrics have a unique charm and attractiveness.

This craft is ageless! It dates back to time immemorial, and yet, today, it is surprisingly new.

I

HISTORICAL BACKGROUND OF
THE CRAFT

TIE-AND-DYE or tie-dyeing is a resist-dyeing process. It consists of knotting, binding, folding or sewing certain parts of the cloth in such a way that when it is dyed the dye cannot penetrate into these areas.

This craft has been practised from very early times by people in many parts of the world. It is uncertain when and where it originated, or whether in the first place resist dyeing was discovered accidentally. The earliest records, from India and Japan, date back to the sixth and seventh centuries A.D. Chinese tie-dyed silks of this period were found in the burial grounds at Astana and at Khotan on the Old Silk Road in Sinkiang, East Turkestan. Traders travelling the old caravan routes throughout Asia, India and the Far East carried tie and dye cloths from one place to another as part of their merchandise.

Fragments of tie-and-dye fabrics were found in the tombs of the ancient Incas of Peru, showing that it was a flourishing craft in that region before the Spanish conquest in the fifteenth century.

In India tie-and-dye was known as " bandhana " work. This has become associated with the small resist or coloured spots, which were arranged to form patterns on a dyed ground. The girls or " bandhani " who tied up the cloths (usually folded into four or six thicknesses) of fine muslin or silk, grew the nails of their thumbs and forefingers very long to enable them to pick up the minute " points " of material to bind with cotton. Also, skilfully executed zig-zag designs were produced by folding and twisting the cloth diagonally before binding.

The craft suffered a great setback towards the end of the nineteenth century when fabric printers sold cheap copies of the actual bandhana designs. About this time the indigo and other vegetable dyes formerly used were replaced by synthetic dyes.

In Japan, the spot technique or " shibori " was widely used

for a variety of cotton and silk fabrics dyed with indigo. Later on folding, rope and sewing methods were developed.

During the Middle Ages China exported many tie-and-dye wares to neighbouring countries. The spot, folding and sewing (known as " tritik ") methods were employed to decorate these cloths. The cottons were usually indigo dyed but the silks were often of many colours.

Indo-China, Thailand and especially Indonesia have been important tie-and-dye areas. The spot and tritik methods were mainly used to decorate the fabrics, usually silk, dyed in gay colours. Bast and leaf fibres were used in Indonesia for sewing and binding.

In many countries the craft is known by the Malay word " plangi."

The tribes of North Africa produced simple spot patterns on their woollen cloths.

The craft is still flourishing up to the present day in the West African countries of Nigeria, Ghana, Liberia, Ivory Coast, Sierra Leone, Dahomey and the Cameroons. The Yoruba women of West Nigeria, where the craft is known as " adire," " adire ido " or " adire alabere," produce magnificent cloths dyed with indigo. These are elaborately patterned by the clump, folding and tritik methods. Raffia and bast are used for sewing and binding.

In the Western Hemisphere, besides those in Peru, pre-Columbian tie-and-dye fabrics have been found in Utah, Arizona and New Mexico of the U.S.A. These were of cotton decorated with resist spots and circles.

The craft was practised at different times in Ecuador, Guatemala, Bolivia, Paraguay, Argentina and Mexico, where fine woollen and cotton hand woven cloths were dyed with spot and tritik patterns.

In Europe a small amount of simple tie-and-dye has been produced in Sweden, Hungary and Czechoslovakia.

[1

THE PROCESS OF TIE-DYEING

THE Process of Tie-dyeing is as follows:
1. Wash cloth to remove dirt, grease or dressing.
2. Iron.
3. Mark out the pattern on the cloth in pencil.
4. Prepare the cloth by knotting, binding, folding, sewing, etc. or a combination of these, always keeping one side as the right side, on the outside of the bundle.
5. Add wax or any thickening agent, if required.
6. Prepare dye and test for colour.
7. Wet sample if necessary and place in the dye for the required length of time.
8. Remove and squeeze out surplus dye.
9. Rinse in the sink or a bowl until the water is clear.
10. Squeeze out surplus water and hang up to dry.
11. When a second or third colour is to be dyed, tie up the sample again or add more binding where the previous colour is to be reserved. Repeat the dyeing process for each subsequent colour. After the final dyeing and rinsing, dry as quickly as possible.
12. Untie the sample.
13. Rinse again if necessary, and partially dry.
14. Iron while still damp.
15. Collect and tie together any lengths of thread which can be used again. Dry them and wrap on a piece of cardboard for future use. Any lengths over six inches are worth saving, and can be used several times.
Keep the coarse and fine binding threads separate.

EQUIPMENT

Very little equipment is needed for tie-dyeing, so that the easier forms of the craft can be readily tried out at home or in the classroom.

The basic needs are:
(a) Vessels to contain the dyes,

13

(*b*) a means of rinsing the dyed sample,

(*c*) somewhere to hang the sample to drip and dry, and, of course,

(*d*) fabrics, dyes and binding thread.

Dye Vessels

These should just comfortably accommodate the tied-up sample, so that it is immersed in the dye, and yet not be so large that an unnecessary amount of dye must be mixed. Saucepans, bowls, basins, buckets, etc. of stainless steel, enamel or galvanised ware can be used for hot and cold dyes; also, for cold dyes, vessels made of plastic, pot and glass can be employed.

Rinsing Facilities

A sink with plenty of water is the ideal way to rinse, but a large bucket or bowl may be used if the water can be changed frequently.

Other items which may be helpful are: Several plastic or old spoons. Sticks or glass rods for stirring the dye. A small pair of scissors with thin blades. Rubber gloves. Darning or crewel needles. Old newspapers. Screw-top jars or bottles to store dye liquid.

Binding Thread (see pages 29, 36, 42, 74, 93)

Dyes (see pages 169–175)

Cloth

Beginners are advised to make the first few experiments with pieces cut from old sheets, shirts and pillow cases. This cloth, which has been well washed, is absorbent and dyes well.

All cotton cloths (especially mercerized) are excellent for tie-and-dye. Ex: lawn, butter muslin, voile, drill, poplin, cambric, casement, all sheeting, flannelette, towelling, cotton velvet, velveteen, corduroy velvet, cotton satin, sateen, repp, calico, unbleached calico, after it has been scoured.

Viscose rayon, linens and hessians, so long as they are absorbent.

Silks: jap, noille, foulard, twill, chiffon, etc. Chlorinated woollens, nun's veiling, georgette, flannel; mixtures such as Viyella, Clydella. Fabrics of man-made fibres can be used if the appropriate dyes are available (manufacturers would supply information).

Wax and Flour Paste

Sometimes, where a pronounced resist is required, the binding alone is not enough to keep out all or most of the dye. In this case it may be reinforced by adding flour paste or wax.

Wax

Place a piece of paraffin wax or half a candle in an old saucepan or tin and heat until it melts. While still hot, paint it over the bindings with a small brush. Immerse the sample in cold dye for several minutes. Rinse thoroughly and dry. Untie and rinse again. Flake off any loose wax. Remove the rest of the wax by placing the sample between sheets of newspaper and pressing with a very hot iron.

Flour Paste

Mix three level teaspoonsful of flour with a little warm water to make a smooth paste. Pour over it $\frac{1}{4}$ pint of boiling water. Boil up if it does not thicken. Apply this paste to the bindings and leave to dry before dyeing. Hot or cold dye may be used.

Protection For The Hands When Binding

When there is a considerable amount of binding to be done, the fingers may need some protection to prevent the thread from cutting into the skin or causing blisters.

A thin cotton glove or mitten can be worn on the hand that takes the greater strain of pulling. If wearing a glove impedes the movement of the fingers, or generally slows down the process of binding, place strips of adhesive plaster over the vulnerable areas of the fingers or hands.

It may be helpful to wrap the thread on a reel or piece of cardboard, which can be gripped when tightening and pulling up the binding.

Another way of easing the strain on the hands when pulling up the binding is to wrap the thread several times round a pencil or similar object, which can then be used as a handle. The pencil is released when the thread is sufficiently taut and the process repeated as further binding requires tightening.

When a large or long sample needs binding, attach thick thread to a stationary object. Then stand some distance away and turn the sample, allowing the taut thread to wrap round the area that requires binding.

Dye can usually be removed from the hands by immersing them for a few seconds in diluted bleach.

Templets

A templet or template is a replica or pattern of a given shape. For the purpose of tie-and-dye it is best made of cardboard, thick strong paper or any similar substance sufficiently rigid for drawing round.

Templets are used for reproducing any motif where an ordinary tracing is impracticable and for marking out the shapes in repetitive designs.

In some techniques, for instance, certain sewn or pleated designs, where the cloth has to be folded double, the templet to be used is the original shape cut in half.

Where a set of measurements has to be marked on the cloth in several places, time can be saved by employing a strip of cardboard or paper, appropriately marked, instead of a ruler.

Quite often, as with a spot pattern, only the layout of the design needs indicating. In this case, plan the arrangement or unit of repeat on strong paper, making for each spot a hole just big enough to insert the point of a pencil. This perforated templet can then be used for transferring the design arrangement on to the fabric, by making a pencil dot in each of the small holes.

Washing the Cloth

All new cloth should be given a hot wash in soap powder, detergent or Lissapol D ($\frac{1}{2}$ teaspoonful per 2 pints) to get rid of grease or dressing. If this presents too many difficulties, as for instance, when dealing with a class of children, it is possible to wash and rinse the tied-up sample. Even to soak it in hot water for a while and then to squeeze and rinse is better than no treatment at all. Most cloths used in schools which are treated ready for printing are excellent for tie-and-dye and do not need the preliminary wash.

III

TEXTURES

AS an introduction to the craft of tie-and-dye, a few experiments with " marbling " are a " must." They are a stimulating and rewarding way of proving to the beginner that when cloth is bunched up closely and bound with thread or string, before being dyed, uneven dyeing, and in some parts complete resistance to the dye, is caused.

Little or no skill is required for this exercise and the results are largely fortuitous, but none the less quite pleasant. It is a valuable means of finding out the effects produced when a second or third colour is dyed over the first.

The variegated and irregular cloud-like texture which is dyed on the cloth by the marbling technique can be quite attractive without further additions, but it provides a rich and unusual background for prints, stencils, embroidery, etc. After the sample has been " marbled " it can be tied up again into a definite design and dyed a darker or contrasting colour so that in the resist areas the marbled texture shows through instead of the plain white cloth. For instance, if large-scale circles are bound up on a previously marbled background and the sample is then dyed a darker colour, the effect produced is one of textured circles on a dark ground.

Method

Take a piece of cloth about the size of a handkerchief, or smaller, and gather it up into a ball or bundle in the palm of the hand, keeping the right side of the cloth to the outside (1). Bind the bundle round and round in all directions with thread or string until it is a hard, solid mass. Fasten off the binding thread, leaving one end about six inches long, which can be held while the bundle is lowered into the dye bath (2).

Immerse the bundle in the dye for a few seconds only. The longer it is left, the more the dye penetrates into the folds of the cloth.

17

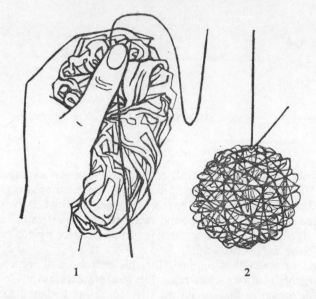

1   2

Squeeze out the surplus dye from the bundle and rinse. Untie before or after drying. If the texture is not evenly distributed, tie up the sample again and dye the same colour as before.

For a second or third colour, repeat the whole process of bunching and tying. Whenever re-tying, try to arrange that the cloth not already textured is placed near the surface, whilst the areas that need no further patterning are tucked away in the centre of the bundle.

If, after this, there are still large patches of cloth that have missed the dye, completely rearrange the bundle so that the bare patches project on the outside. Bind, and dye again, or apply the dye with a brush. Previously dyed thread may be used for the binding (see page 36).

TWISTING AND COILING

This texture is more definite in character than marbling and is more evenly spaced over the cloth. Whereas marbling can be employed to dye specific areas of a sample, the whole length of cloth must be immersed in the dye, when making a texture by the twisting and coiling technique.

Method

Keeping the right side outside, bring the two selvedge edges of the cloth together to form a tube lengthways (3). Gather up each end of the tube and tie separately with thread. For a smaller sample this is not so essential. An end can be held in either hand while the tube is twisted into a cord (4). Another method is to attach one end to a stationary object, then proceed to twist the tube (5) until it begins to coil back on itself to make a cord.

6   7   8   9

Fold the tube in half (6) and tie the two ends together. Regulate the coils of the cord (7). Bind round the cord, beginning and finishing at the open end (8).

Dye for a few seconds. Squeeze out surplus dye, rinse and dry. Before untying, further binding may be added and a second colour dyed (9).

The two ends of the cord may be dyed different colours.

Rinse, dry and untie.

If the texture is not well distributed, the tying up may be repeated—arranging the undyed parts on the outside—and the sample dyed as before.

IV

KNOTTING

ONE of the easiest and quickest ways of producing a dyed texture is to tie a length of cloth into knots. This can be tied in several ways, depending on the size, shape and grain of the cloth. Fine fabrics such as muslin, butter muslin, lawn, fine cambric, georgette, voile, silk and nylon are ideal for this technique. Coarse-grained, bulky fabric is definitely unsuitable. Knotting may be operated in three ways, viz.:

1. A length of cloth tied into knots.
2. A square, rectangle or triangle of cloth knotted.
3. Knots tied in a length of cloth to form an all-over pattern.

1. A LENGTH OF CLOTH TIED INTO KNOTS

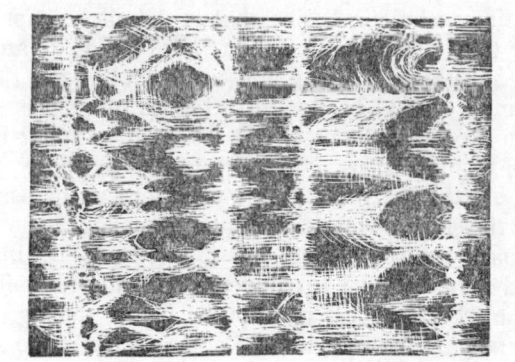

A strip of fine cloth is best; the wider and coarser it is, the fewer the knots. The most interesting texture is obtained from more and smaller knots rather than large, clumsy ones.

Method

It is necessary, first of all, to make a test knot at one end of the sample to see how much cloth it takes up. After tying make a crease or mark just beyond it. Untie the knot and measure the

21

distance between the mark or crease and the end of the cloth. It can now be estimated how many knots to tie on the sample. Rule a pencil line across the cloth where the centre of each knot is planned (10).

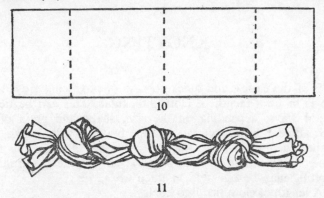

10

11

It is advisable to tie the knots in the middle of the sample first, then work outwards. Twist the cloth into a roll and tie a knot at each pencil line. Tighten up the knots by manipulating the fabric until they are reasonably uniform in size (11).

Immerse the cloth in the dye for a short time. Rinse and dry. The knotting technique is one that is definitely improved by a second or third dyeing so that the texture builds up and acquires form and substance. This applies to all three types of knotting.

The sample should be bone dry before untying is attempted. A wooden skewer, bone crochet hook or any similar fine, blunt-ended object may be used to prise the knots loose. On no account should the sharp metal points of scissors be used for this, otherwise the sample will develop numerous holes and tears. The untying may take some time, but if the knots are manipulated between the thumbs and forefingers they will gradually slacken. Repeat the whole process of knotting before dyeing the second colour, arranging the next lot of knots in exactly the same position as the previous ones.

2. A SQUARE, RECTANGLE OR TRIANGLE KNOTTED

Square or Rectangle

Method

Pick up a point of cloth in the middle of the sample. Smooth it down in the left hand, twisting and curling it until a knot can be tied (12). Tie each of the corners into three or four smaller knots (13) (14) (15).

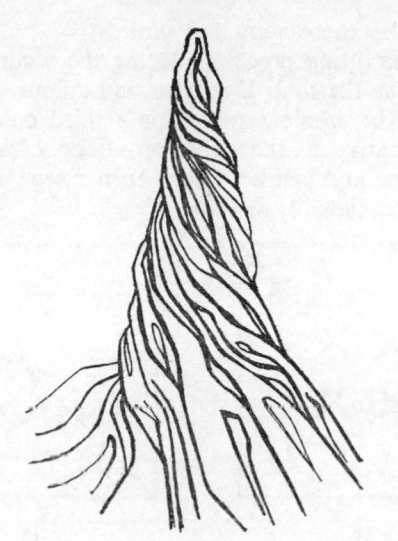

12

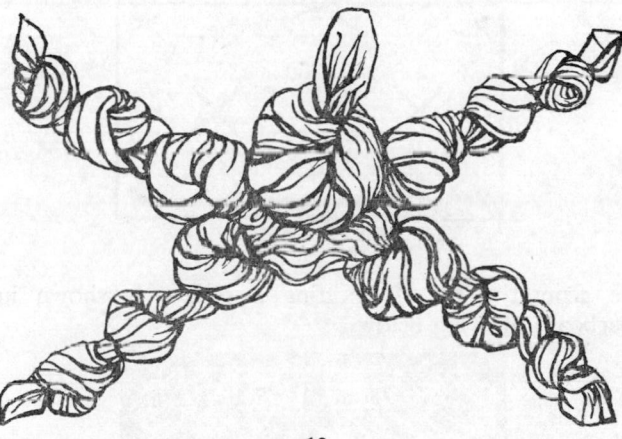

13

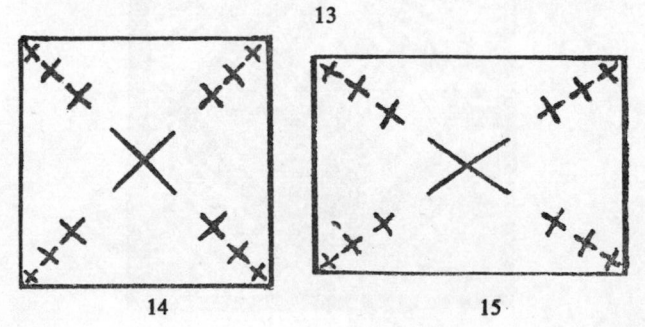

14   15

Dye, rinse, dry thoroughly and untie.

Repeat the knotting process, placing the second knots in the same position as the first. Dye a second colour. Rinse, dry and untie. Repeat the whole process for a third colour.

As an alternative to the above grouping of knots, omit the large central one and just knot each corner several times (16), or as (17), or fold diagonally as (18).

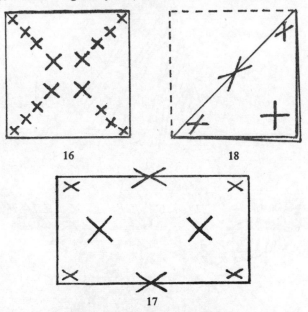

16   18

17

The general effect of knotting a square is shown in the scraperboard drawing below.

Triangle

The main knot can be tied at the apex (19), or at the centre of one of the sides of the triangle (20) and then the three pointed corners tied into two, three or four knots.

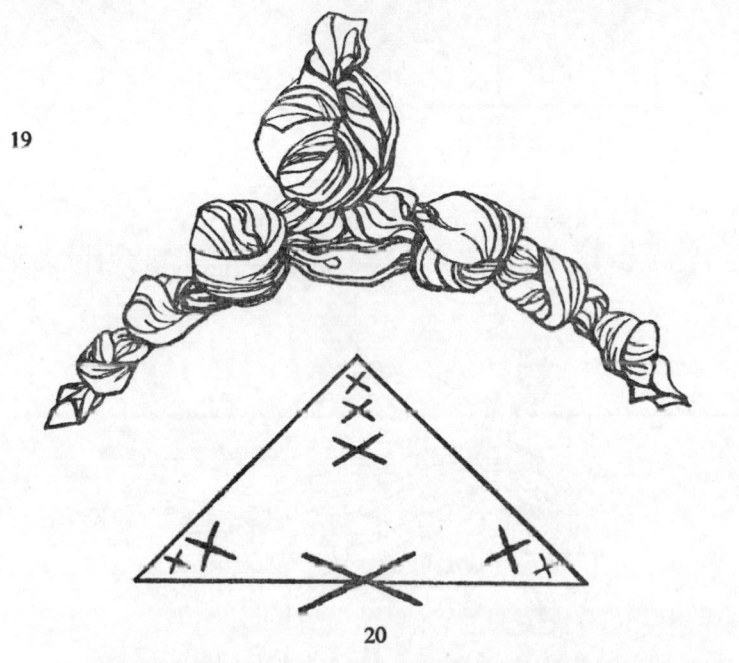

Alternatively, the three points of the triangle only need be knotted, leaving the centre unpatterned, or as (21) (22), or the triangle folded in half (23) (24).

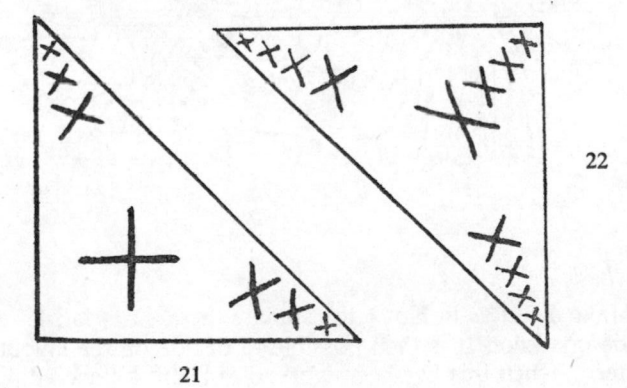

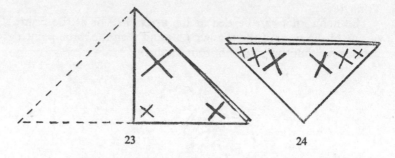

23   24

3. KNOTTING TO FORM AN ALL-OVER PATTERN

Fabric of the finest weave is essential for this type of knotting.

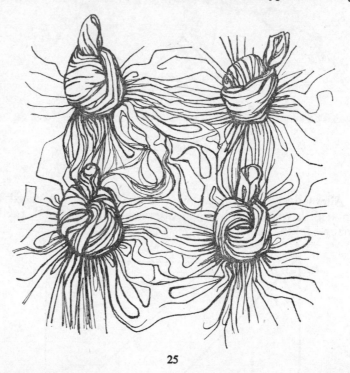

25

Method

Make a test as in No. 1 to estimate the area of fabric required to tie one knot. It is then possible to decide on the layout of the pattern. When this has been worked out, put a pencil dot on the cloth to indicate the centre of each knot. Pick up a point of cloth at each dot and smooth it between the thumb and fingers with a pull down the warp and weft of the fabric. Curl it round and tie into a knot (12). To tighten up each knot, hold the little tuft in the middle, whilst sliding and manœuvring the fabric towards it.

When the knotting has been completed (25), dye, rinse and dry thoroughly. Untie and re-tie before dyeing another colour.

Variations

1. The individual knots or tufts may be dipped in a colour different from that of the background. This way of tying up the cloth produces a circular variegated patch of texture.

2. To ring the changes, some of the knots may be tied as follows—producing a diamond shape.

Method

Mark the position of the knots. Crease the fabric lengthwise for several inches on either side of the dot, parallel to the selvedge. Pick up the folded edge of cloth at the pencil dot—see (68) (69)—and smooth it firmly into a long pointed cone, giving an extra pull where the fabric is on the cross. Curl it round and tie into a knot. Tighten this into a hard, firm knob.

Dye, rinse, dry and untie.

When retying for another colour, repeat the round knots and diamond knots in their respective positions. The pattern is more interesting when both shapes are incorporated.

3. The area of texture produced by one knot can be made larger by adjusting the size of the tuft of cloth which projects from the centre like an ear. A bigger tuft and a loose knot give a larger shape, and vice versa (26).

4. When very fine fabric is used, the central tuft can be so elongated that it is possible to tie another smaller knot beyond the first, making a double-deck effect (27). The smaller one can be dyed a different colour from the larger one.

5. Before finally untying, the knots can all be gathered into a cluster and held outside the dyebath while the background is dyed a different colour.

6. Another variation may be made by tying up alternate knots only. Dye, rinse but do *not* untie. Tie the remaining knots and dye the second colour. Rinse and dry. Untie all the knots.

Now tie up all the knots on the sample and dye a third colour. Rinse, dry and untie.

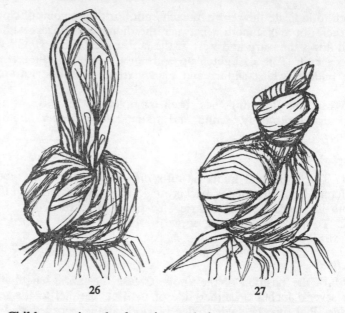

26   27

Children trying the knotting technique may find the untying a little difficult. In this case leave the knots slacker and reinforce them with binding to create a satisfactory resist. Then "wet-out" the sample before dyeing.

Sometimes it is easier to untie the knots while the sample is immersed in water; but first rinse thoroughly. Another way to ease the untying is to twist the cloth emerging from either side of the knot, back into it, as if turning a screw. This should be done when the sample is dry.

V

BINDING

BINDING is one of the most important processes in tie-and-dye, used either alone or as a supplement to other methods. If certain parts of the fabric are bound very tightly with thread before being dyed, they will resist the dye partially or completely. Binding applied before the first dyeing reserves the original cloth (usually white). Binding applied before the second dyeing reserves the first colour. Binding applied before the third dyeing reserves the second colour, etc.

Linen thread Nos. 18, 35 and 45 are excellent for binding, but cotton, Sylko, string, cord, yarn, raffia, tape, bast, rubber rings, etc., can be used. Obviously a stronger binding thread must be used where the tension or strain is greater; a thicker one when covering large resist areas and also for coarser cloth. Cotton or thinner thread may often be used for smaller and shallower tying and for finer materials.

Flour and water paste may be added to the bindings where necessary to help form a crisper resist. To get a solid resist area with well-defined, sharp edges, paint melted wax over the whole binding to exclude the dye completely. A cold dye must then be used.

It is possible to bind with waxed thread, or ordinary carpet thread can be treated by sliding it over a solid lump of hard wax.

It is absolutely essential that the binding should remain firm and taut, and that no slackening off should occur during the dyeing operation, for it must keep the cloth bunched up so closely that the dye cannot penetrate into the folds. Binding, however well accomplished, is ineffective if the fastening off is not absolutely secure.

FASTENING-OFF METHODS

When commencing an area of binding, always keep the beginning of the thread free for at least two inches (28), so that when the binding is finished, the other end of the thread can be brought back to this spot (29) and both ends tied together securely (30).

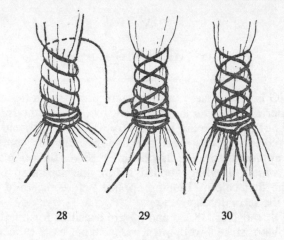

28   29   30

To Retain an End of Thread for Fastening Off

There are two ways of doing this :

(a) Hold the sample in the left hand with the thumb adjoining the area that requires binding. Place the beginning of the binding thread between the thumb and the cloth (31). Wrap the rest

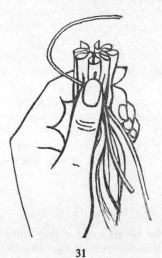

31

of the thread round the sample several times, pull it up tightly (32), then release the end from under the thumb and tie the two pieces of thread together (33, 34). Leaving the original end of thread free, continue the binding in this area (28), pulling it as tightly as possible.

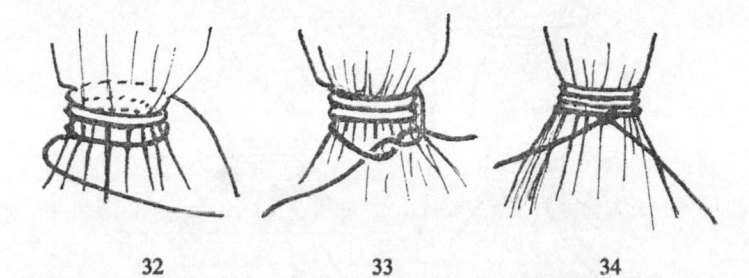

32   33   34

(*b*) When tying on the binding thread, retain an end and weave it between the fingers of the left hand before commencing to bind (35). Grip the end firmly between the second and third fingers until the binding is completed, when it will be available for fastening off (36).

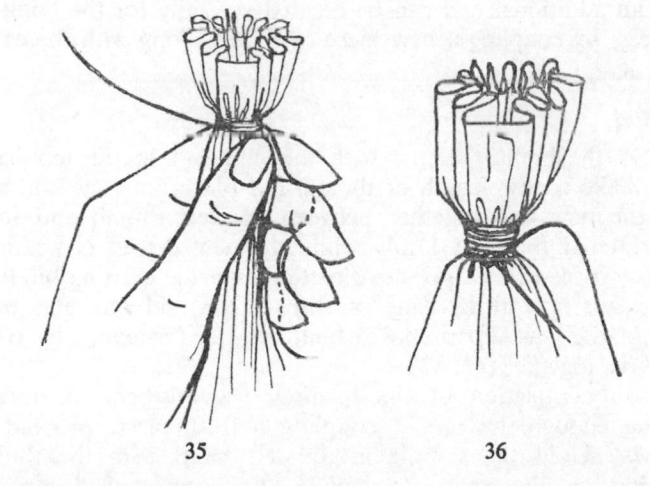

35   36

Tying Threads for Fastening Off

The most satisfactory means of fastening off after binding, maintaining the tension meanwhile, is to tie one end of the thread to the other, or to another thread. Tie the two threads once (33), then pull up both ends again before completing the knot (34). Where there are several ends, tie them in pairs, or, if an odd number occurs (37), tie three together (38).

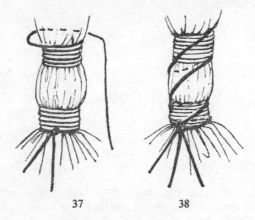

37   38

Making an Extra End of Thread for Tying

Sometimes after the binding has been finished an isolated end of thread needs a second one to form a secure knot. In this case an additional end can be created specially for the tying-up process, by coupling a new piece of thread along with the existing one.

Method

Hold the bound sample with the odd end in the left hand (39). Take a new length of thread and place both the odd end and the new end together between the left thumb and forefinger. Hold the ends firmly while the new thread is wrapped once or twice in the opposite direction over the existing binding. There are now three ends of thread, the odd one and both ends of the new superimposed binding (40). Fasten off by tying the three together (41, 42).

If on completion of the binding, the odd end of thread is long enough, instead of coupling a fresh piece, proceed as follows: Hold the sample in the left hand with the thumb pressing on the area of binding just completed. Loop the thread round the first finger of the left hand, then return it over the existing binding, in the reverse direction, once or twice (43, 44). Release the loop from the finger and use it as the second end for tying the fastening-off knot (45).

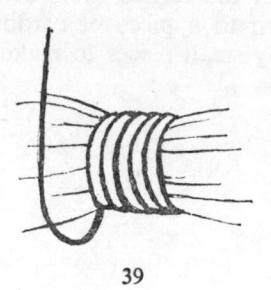

39

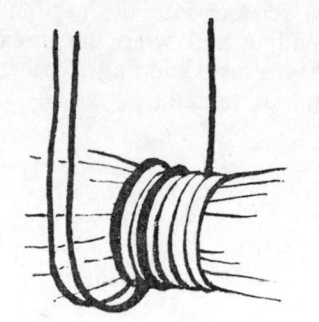

40

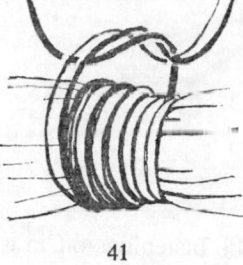

41

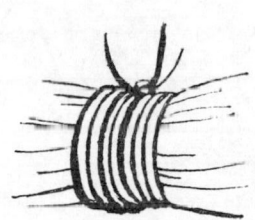

42

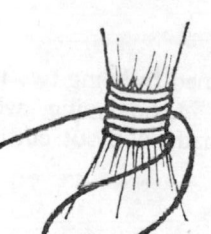

43

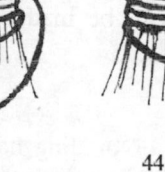

44

45

Untying

It is very risky trying to cut into the middle of an area of binding. In cutting the threads, a hole can so easily be cut in the fabric.

When the sample is ready to be untied, look for the two ends that were knotted together when fastening off. Pull these away from the sample, so that a small triangular gap is created between the knot and the rest of the binding. Insert the points

3—TAD * *

of the scissors into the gap and cut the thread (46). Unwind the binding and wrap the thread on to a piece of cardboard for further use, knotting together any small pieces to make one continuous thread.

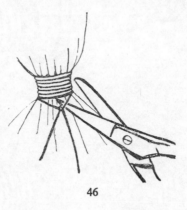

46

To be workmanlike, arrange all the fastenings-off in a certain position (129). This will speed up the untying.

A Slip Knot

Although not as stable as a knot formed by tying two threads together, the slip knot has its uses in tie-dyeing, where a succession of small bindings can be made without cutting the thread.

Method

When the required amount of binding has been added, hold the sample in the left hand close to the neck of binding. Wrap the binding thread in an anti-clockwise direction, round the first two or three fingers or the thumb of the left hand (47, 48). With the right hand, ease the loop gradually off the fingers or thumb (47a, 48a), and over the tuft of cloth above the neck of binding (47b), turning it over so that the length of thread is underneath (47c, 48b). Pull the thread taut so that the loop grips firmly round the existing binding (49). Make a second or third slip knot, one over the other, if extra tension needs to be maintained.

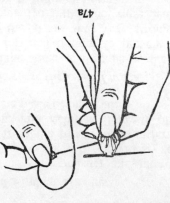

47

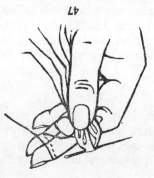

47a

47b

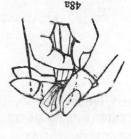

47c

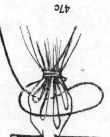

48

48a

48b

49

Dyed Binding Threads

Some very unusual and interesting results are achieved by binding cloth with previously dyed thread. Small flecks of dye from the thread are transferred to the design, giving extra colour and richness. Threads of several colours can be used on one piece of material.

To Prepare the Dyed Thread

Make some small coils or skeins of string, thread or cotton. Tie top and bottom to prevent them from becoming tangled. Dip the skeins into very strong dye liquor. Squeeze out the surplus dye, but do not rinse. Hang up, or place on some newspaper, to drain and dry.

Wrap the thread round a piece of cardboard to keep it in good condition until it is needed.

Thread bought on a card can be dyed without further preparation. Dyed thread must *not* be rinsed before it is used for binding.

TYPES OF BINDING

Although the dyed pattern is affected by the kind of binding thread used, the way in which the binding is done plays a much more important role.

Different effects may be obtained as follows:

1. A "**Band**" of very close, solid binding in a single or double layer (50, 51), should give a complete resist over that area.

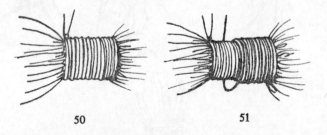

50   51

2. "**Criss-cross**" or "**Lattice**" (52), "**Spiral**" or "**Open**" (53) binding gives a partial resist, with a texture that echoes the mesh-work of the binding threads. After the first dyeing, areas of No. 1 or No. 3 can be superimposed over No. 2.

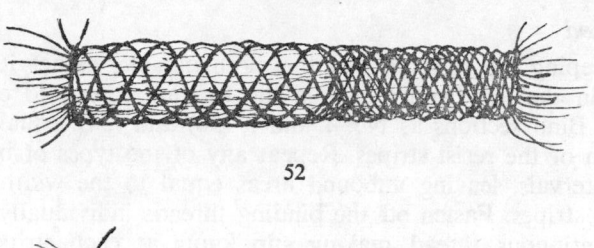

52

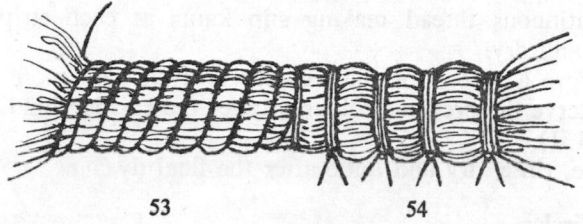

53   54

3. A "Line" or tight narrow binding gives a very thin resist
    stripe (54).

The amount of dye allowed to penetrate through the cloth
is controlled by the tightness or slackness of the bindings and
length of dyeing time.

PATTERNS MADE WITH BINDING

(a) Stripes or Bands

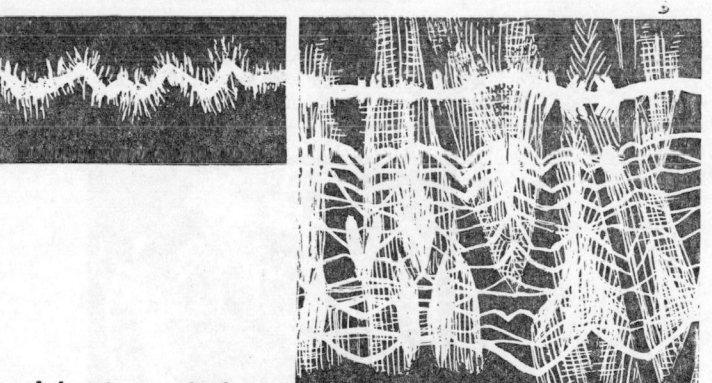

Line binding

Band made by criss-cross binding

By this method a resist stripe with an irregular edge is
produced, the area in between the bands of binding being the
width of the dyed stripe.

Method

Keeping the right side of the cloth outside, gather it into a roll in the left hand (35). Tie the binding thread to one end (36). Bind sections as No. 1 and 3 (50) and (54), equal to the width of the resist stripes. Repeat any of the types of bindings at intervals, leaving unbound areas equal to the width of the dyed stripes. Fasten off the binding threads individually or use a continuous thread making slip knots at each stripe. Dye, rinse and dry.

Before a second or third colour is dyed, add more binding to reserve the previous colour or alter the existing bindings (see 130, 131).

Dye, rinse, dry and untie after the final dyeing.

(b) Circles

This technique is adaptable for any kind of fabric.

Above left: *Small circle bound with Sylko*
Right: *Small circle with more solid binding*
Below: *Large circle with line and criss-cross binding*

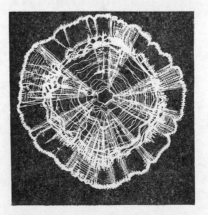

Method

Put a pencil dot to mark the centre of each circle. Pick up a point of cloth at each dot (55) and smooth it with the left hand until it is like a closed umbrella (56). Tie on the binding thread some way from the central point for a large circle (57) but just below it for a small circle (58, 59). The

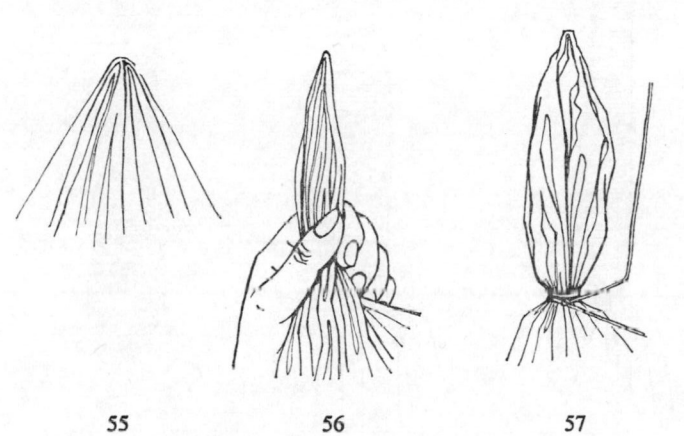

55   56   57

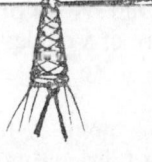

58   59

distance from the central point to the extreme edge of the binding determines the radius of the resist circle. Bind each circle separately with solid (60), criss-cross (61) or line binding, or a combination of all types (62). Fasten off all binding threads, dye as planned and after the final rinse dry and untie.

To cover a circle with criss-cross binding it is best to work in several layers. Tie on the thread (57), make a layer of open binding diagonally up to the central point, then a second layer back over it in the opposite direction, tightening the thread meanwhile. Repeat this up and down binding once or twice, pulling the thread so that each layer is tighter and firmer than the previous one.

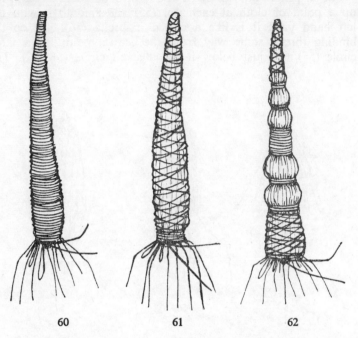

60   61   62

How to reserve an area of total resist whether white or dyed, in the centre of a circle:

Method

Pick up a point X for the centre of the circle on the *wrong* side of the fabric. Bind XY, the required resist area (63a). On

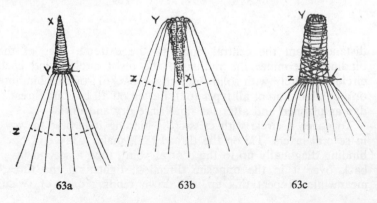

63a   63b   63c

the right side of the sample turn the cloth down at Y so that XY is completely enclosed (63b). Bind YZ, the outer edge of the circle (63c). Dye as required.

Although the circle is an easy technique, patterns of tremendous variety can be achieved by exploiting different arrangements and colour schemes, and by contrasting large and small or textured and plain shapes.

Many diverse effects can be produced in the dyeing process. With one dyeing (blue) :

1. Dye sample as 57 with one line binding=a white ring on a blue ground.
2. Invert the point only, beyond the binding=a blue circle on a white ground.
3. Dye cloth below the binding only=a white circle, on a blue ground.

With a second dyeing (red) :

1st dyeing (blue)	2nd dyeing (red)		Colour of Circle	Colour of Ground
No. 1	No. 2	=	purple	blue
No. 1	No. 3	=	blue	purple
No. 2	No. 1	=	purple	red
No. 2	No. 3	=	blue	red
No. 3	No. 1	=	red	purple
No. 3	No. 2	=	red	blue

When the line binding is tight enough there will be white edges to all these circles. Add binding to get a textured edition of the above results. Binding can be added or removed at each stage giving a still wider range of patterns. The tips can be bleached or dyed another colour, or an extra colour can be applied with a brush.

See also chapter XII on multicolour dyeing.

For a more accurate circle draw the outline in pencil and run a line of tacking stitches round it. Pull up the thread, then pick up the central point and bind as described.

Circles on a sample can be dyed individually and thus differently. After separate treatment, more binding can be added to the circles and the entire sample dyed.

Line bindings placed at intervals below the central point produce a series of concentric circles.

(c) Spots

Left: *Small round and diamond shaped spots, spot with larger central dyed area*
Right: *An irregular resist ring, see Diag. 66a*

A fine fabric is definitely needed for this method, otherwise it is difficult to give precision to the small shapes produced. When a very tiny spot is being tied up a much finer thread, for example sewing cotton or Sylko, should be used for binding.

Method

Put a pencil dot on the cloth where each spot is planned. With a needle pick up a minute portion of cloth on the first dot (64a). Wrap the cotton once or twice round the cloth immediately below the needle (64b). Tie the two ends of cotton, then complete the binding. If the binding is kept close to the needle a tiny spot will be formed. In this case it is safer to leave the needle in place until the spot has been bound and tied (65). A larger resist shape will appear if the " neck " of binding is made broader.

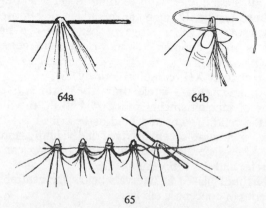

64a   64b

65

Instead of using a needle, the centre of the spot may be picked up with the thumb and forefinger before binding. Both ways should be tried to see which is easier or gives better results.

A slip knot can be used for fastening off after binding each spot. Carry the cotton from one spot to the next without cutting (65, 66).

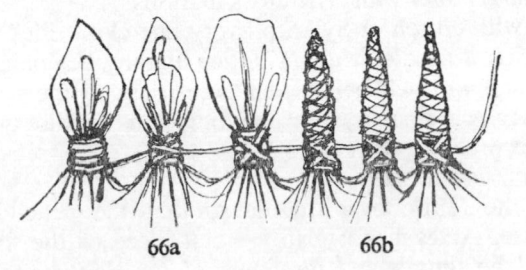

66a   66b

Dye, rinse and dry.

When more than one colour is planned, some of the spots can be tied up after the first colour has been dyed; another layer of binding can be added to the ones already bound; or some of the previously bound spots untied.

Dye, rinse and dry thoroughly before untying.

There will always be a small dyed patch in the centre of each spot unless wax or flour paste is painted on the extreme tip before dyeing.

This central dyed area can be enlarged, so that the resist spot in fact becomes a resist ring (58, 66a).

When undoing very small spots (65), the binding may be eased off the points of cloth without cutting the thread. This operation must be done very gently and with the greatest care, otherwise the cloth will tear.

Using both hands, grip the sample between the thumbs and forefingers on either side of, and right close to, each spot in turn. Pull very warily until the binding begins to move and gradually slips free, over the tip of the spot. Never pull the cloth in the direction of the grain, that is, do not pull along the warp or weft. The secret of success is to pull very gently on the " cross " so that the cloth stretches but does not tear.

Variations

1. *A double, treble or multiple* " spot " can be achieved by picking up the appropriate number of centres on the needle and binding them together as a single unit (67).

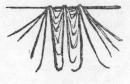

67

2. *A larger spot* with criss-cross markings.

Bind with cotton or Sylko on very fine cloth. Pick up a point of cloth on a needle. Make a lattice binding beginning approximately half an inch below and take it up to the needle. Bind back over the first layer of binding and tie the two ends of cotton securely together as (59).

3. *An irregular spot.*

Fold the fabric over double so that the pencil dot is on the crease. At each dot grip a small piece of the folded cloth between the thumb and forefinger of the right hand (68), pull out (69) and bind the little bunch of cloth (70, 71) and make a slip knot. The thread can be carried on from one spot to the next without cutting (66b).

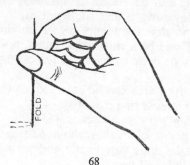

68

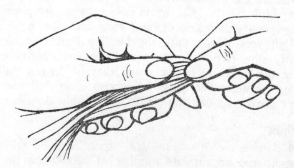

69

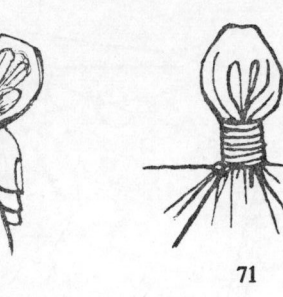

70   71

4. *An irregular " resist " ring.*

This is made in the same way as the irregular spot, except that the binding is confined to a very narrow line, allowing the dye to penetrate to the centre of the shape (66a).

5. *A Lozenge or Diamond-shaped Spot.*

A little practice is needed to get the knack of this important variation on the circular dot.

Fold the material (72), then into four thicknesses so that the dot which represents the centre of the lozenge is at the tip of the double fold (73). Make a secure binding just below the dot. Insert a needle through the dot if it helps in making a firm binding (74). The width of this binding decides the size of the lozenge.

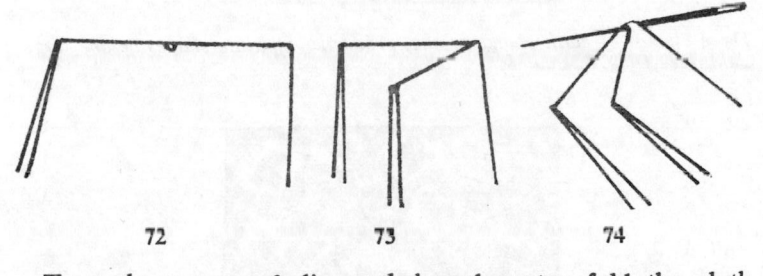

72   73   74

To make a row of diamond-shaped spots : fold the cloth over double, along the required line of spots. Pin or tack in place if necessary. Put pencil dots to denote the position of the spots.

At the first spot, fold the double cloth over again as just described, making four thicknesses (73). Make a binding just below the dot which is situated at the tip of the right-angled corner thus formed (74). Repeat this process at each dot, taking the thread from one to the next without cutting (75) Make a double slip knot at each spot.

Dye as required.

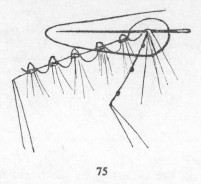

75

It is possible to make a round or diamond-shaped spot by gently pulling the cloth while binding. Pull down and across the grain to produce a circular spot, and on the cross of the cloth to make a diamond spot.

Clump Tying

Three clumps of cloth bound as one, producing separate shapes or one large clump (see Diag. 82 and 83)

Clumps of varying sizes in one design. Large clump had a double binding (Diag. 84)

This method derives its name from the little bunches or clumps that are formed by tying up the material. The cloth itself is bunched, or arranged in various ways and bound, or small objects such as seeds, peas, beans, corn grains, pebbles, shells, corks (76), beads, buttons (77), cotton reels, or pieces of wood, etc. are tied in the fabric.

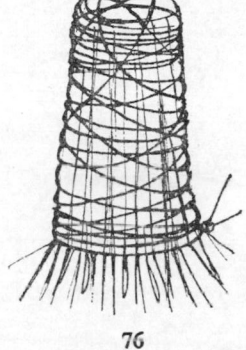

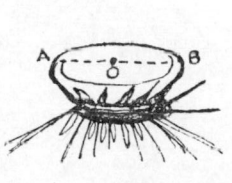

76   77

This technique is widely practised in West Africa, where seeds such as guinea corn are commonly used. Large rectangular cloths are elaborately decorated, often with designs which have a religious significance. There is usually a big central motif, then several bands of pattern stretching across, and finally a border design. These cloths, which are blue and white, are dyed from the indigo grown and prepared in the district. They are used for decorating the local shrines, or are worn as garments, draped round the body.

Method (*a*) Bunching the cloth.

Mark out the design by putting dots to represent each clump. Pick up a piece of cloth on a needle at the first dot (78), make a

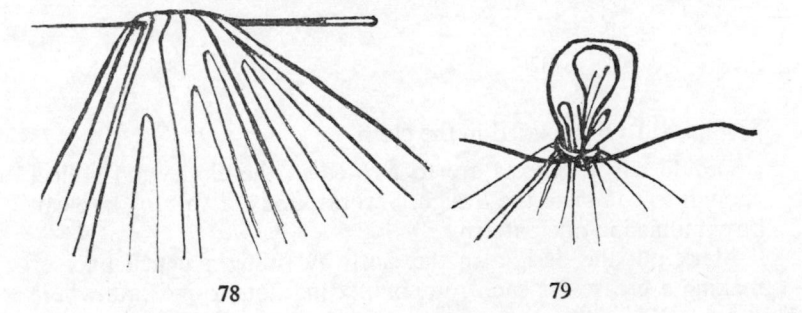

78   79

neck of binding and tie a knot (79). Take the thread along to the next dot to bind the second clump (80), and so on along the line, making a slip knot at each clump (81). Two, three or four clumps can be picked up (82) and bound as one (83). If these are close enough together they will combine to form one larger, more elongated resist shape.

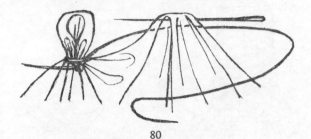

80

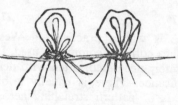

81

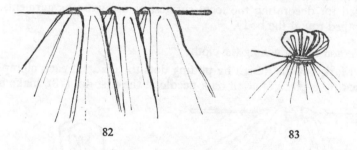

82   83

Method (*b*) Objects tied in the cloth.

Decide which objects are to be tied in the cloth, and collect enough to complete the design. Several kinds of varying size can be combined in one pattern.

Mark out the design on the cloth by ruling a pencil line, or making a crease for each row, or putting dots to indicate where each individual clump is to be made. The dots should be far enough apart to allow the cloth to wrap round each object. It may be advisable to make a trial clump beforehand, to see exactly how much cloth is required for this purpose.

Begin at one end of a row. Place an object under the cloth at the first dot (77 O), or so that the pencil line comes across the middle (77 A B). Bind underneath the object which is now enclosed in the cloth (77). Tie a knot with the binding thread (79). Place the next object in position, bring the binding thread along from the first clump (80) and bind without cutting the thread. Make a slip knot. Continue along the line, inserting and binding an object and making a slip knot at each dot. If there are no dots along the pencil line or crease, pack the objects as closely together as possible.

Where a spiral or circular pattern is to be made, begin tying the objects in the cloth at the centre of the design. When tying up a design on a rectangular piece of cloth, work from one side to the other, or from the centre outwards. Never tie objects round the outside first, otherwise it is very difficult to manipulate the ones in the centre. When there is a very pronounced " neck " (77) and the clumps are close together, the binding will keep taut without making a slip knot. After binding an object in the cloth, carry the thread across to the next clump, making sure it does not sag loosely in between. The advantage of this comes in the untying stage, as the binding can be so easily unwound and wrapped on a piece of cardboard for future use.

When the tying up is completed, immerse the sample for a short time, rinse, dry and untie. Clump tying is a technique which gives good results with one dyeing—preferably in a strong rich colour.

Suggested Variations

1. Tie the clumps with previously dyed thread.
2. Use varying thicknesses of thread.
3. After the first colour has been dyed, add more binding to some of the clumps and dye a second colour.
4. Leave some of the clumps untied for the first dyeing. Tie these in the cloth before the second or third colour is dyed.
5. Paint a contrasting colour on the tops of the clumps.
6. To produce a two-coloured background, after tying up the clumps and dyeing, bunch up the entire sample and bind, as for marbling. Dye a second colour, rinse, dry and untie.

7. Vary the width of the necks of binding (71) or make a double binding, one below the other (84).

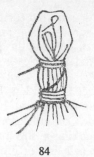

84

8. Design the pattern to give variety by using different shaped objects, vary the spacing, or combine large and minute objects in one design.

9. Telescope several objects one above the other. First, bind a very small object in the cloth, then below that bind a slightly bigger one, and so on (85). Each layer can be dyed a different colour.

85

10. Pleat the cloth before binding it over the object.

11. Texture the cloth before binding it over the objects.

12. Experiment with bleach (see ch. XIV). Keep the bleach from spotting the rest of the sample. Finally, rinse the whole sample thoroughly.

Clump tying may be developed and elaborated to form some of the most exciting patterns possible in tie-dyeing.

The three main factors contributing to the formation of these are :

(*a*) The arrangement of the cloth.

This may be pleated, sewn or draped, etc., beforehand, or it may be manipulated on or around a base.

(*b*) Binding.

Types of thread, which can be very varied, as well as the density of the binding, play an important role in determining the formation of the texture. This is only produced in those areas where the binding grips the cloth to the base tightly enough to form a resist.

(*c*) Bases or backgrounds.

The function of these is to support the manipulated cloth, providing areas where binding can be applied to form resists. The shape, symmetrical or irregular, the size and the texture of the bases affects the finished pattern. Pieces of wood, large stones, chunks of cork, plastic articles are all ideal.

Any areas that are so flat that the binding does not grip enough to produce a resist, need padding out with a thick layer of newspaper (as in 241). Take the binding in all directions over and around the enclosed base.

Polythene

An interesting resist is obtained when small pieces of polythene are tied round clumps of cloth before dyeing. Polythene is also useful for covering those parts that need protecting from the dye or for tying over small areas that have been dyed, so that they do not stain the rest of the sample.

VI

FOLDING

MANY striking patterns and effects, especially stripes, are produced by the folding technique, combined with binding.

To get the best results, this method calls for very accurate workmanship. Generally speaking, very narrow stripes should be confined to the finer fabrics, but most kinds of material can be used for medium to wide stripes.

Cotton and thread are suitable for binding fine cloths, but a stronger thread or string is preferable for coarse material or wide stripes.

A bulky tied-up sample should be left longer in the dye-bath so that the dye can penetrate to the inner folds.

There are four main categories that come under this heading :
1. Simple stripes.
2. An individual or edge stripe.
3. Folded squares.
4. Rope tying.

1. SIMPLE STRIPES

This is a quick and easy way to dye stripes on a length of cloth to use as a background for prints, stencils, embroidery, etc., or as the first stage of a tie-dye design where a pattern of a more precise nature is to be superimposed.

1a. Two Resist Stripes.

Fold the fabric in half, in the direction of the stripe (86). Form the sample into a bundle of accordion pleats at right angles to the first fold (87, 88). These need not be too precise. Make a solid band of binding round the bundle (89). Dye. During the process of dyeing, open out the pleats to allow the dye to reach the inner folds (90). This applies to all the folding methods. Rinse and dry. Add more binding before dyeing a second colour (91). Rinse, dry and untie.

Pleats on one side of a binding can be dyed a different colour from those on the other side (92).

FOLDING

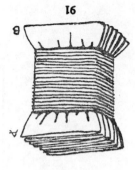

91

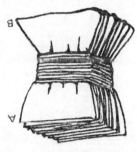

89

92

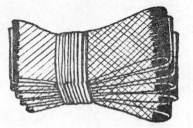

90

88

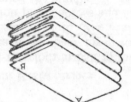

86

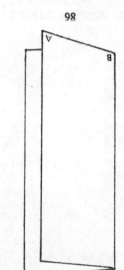

87

Slightly different stripes are made if the binding completely encloses one end of the bundle (93, 94). Add more binding when dyeing a second colour (95, 96).

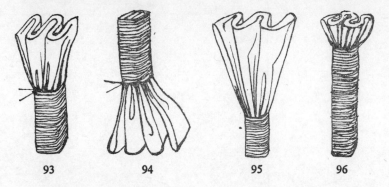

93   74   95   96

1b. Four Resist Stripes

Fold the cloth in half in the direction of the proposed stripes. Turn each side back again to the middle so that there are four thicknesses of cloth (97). Make the folded cloth into a series of accordion pleats across and at right angles to the previous ones. Bind round the bundle (87, 88, 89).

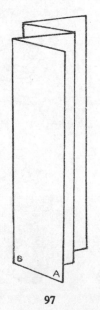

97

Dye as already described (p. 52).

From this it will be apparent that the number of times the sample is folded in the first place determines the number of resist stripes produced.

1c. A Larger Number of Stripes

Rule a line for the middle of each stripe and crease. Fold the creased edges together like accordion pleats (98). Make another set of pleats at right angles to the first ones (99). Bind the middle of the bundle (100) and dye, opening out the folds so that the dye can penetrate right up to the binding (90). Leave longer in the dyebath. Rinse and dry.

98

99

100

Add more binding when dyeing a second or third colour. Dye the tips of the folded edges another colour if necessary (92).

Rinse, dry and untie.

1d. Remove binding; then make a fresh one at right angles down the bundle (101). Dye a second colour.

1e. Before untying the bundle, a band of binding can be made across the first binding and at right angles to it (102). Dye a different colour, rinse, dry and untie.

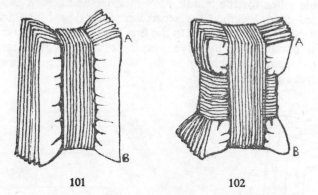

101   102

2. AN INDIVIDUAL OR EDGE STRIPE

By this method a single stripe, narrow or wide and of more than one colour, can be dyed on a length of cloth, or a number of stripes, similar or dissimilar, can be dyed separately on a sample.

Narrow edge stripe

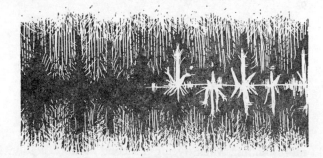

Wider stripe with (right) extreme edges bleached

These stripes can be placed in any direction on the cloth, horizontally, vertically or diagonally. They may be parallel to each other or placed at random.

After dyeing a series of parallel stripes in one direction, a second layer can be made at right angles to the first to form a plaid or trellis effect.

2a. Dyeing a Single Edge Stripe

Method

Rule a line on the cloth, to indicate the centre of the stripe, and make a fold along it (103). Beginning at the right-hand side crease this folded edge into small zig-zag pleats with the thumbs and forefingers (104, 105). Keep the top edges absolutely level.

There should now be a bundle of accordion pleats (106).

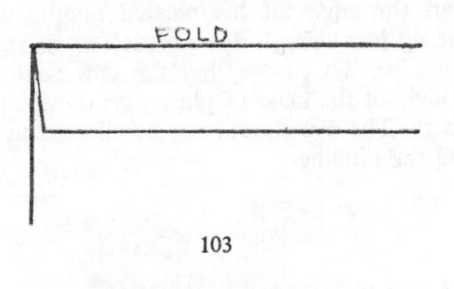

FOLD

103

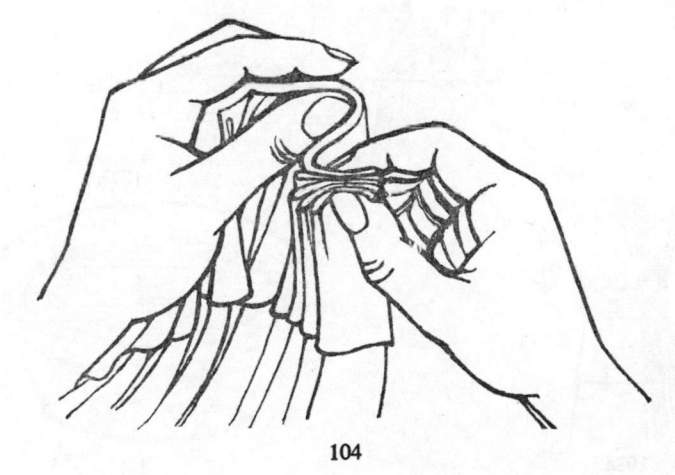

104

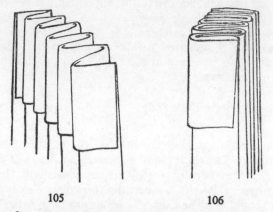

105   106

Place a firm line of binding round the bundle at a distance from the edge equal to half the width of the proposed stripe (107a). Invert the edges of the pleated bundle into a shallow bowl containing just enough dye to reach up as far as the binding (108a and b). To ensure that the dye rises as far as the binding throughout the mass of pleats, gently open out the folds near the centre. The dye should not be allowed to spread to the cloth beyond the binding.

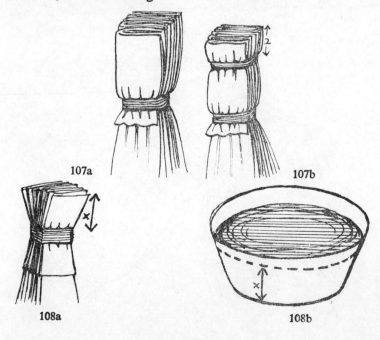

107a   107b

108a   108b

When the dyeing is completed, if rubber gloves are worn, it is possible to extract the surplus dye by squeezing or pressing the dyed area of the sample against the side of the bowl (109). Rinse the small dyed area immediately and squeeze in a piece of old clean rag or newspaper to absorb the excess moisture.

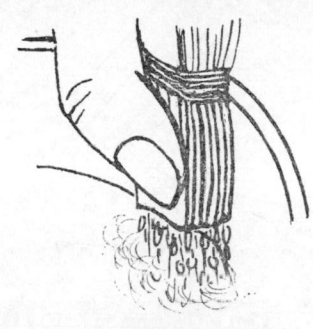

109

For a second colour add more binding nearer the edges (107b) (2) and dye in the same way as the first (107a, 108, 109).

The extreme edges can be dyed a third colour, either by pressing them on a cloth impregnated with dye, or by applying the dye with a brush.

After dyeing, the edges of the pleats can be dipped in bleach. Rinse thoroughly before and after untying. Wax may be painted on the tips of the pleats before the first or second dyeing.

Rinse, dry and untie.

2b. Several Stripes

When several stripes are planned, mark their positions on the cloth, then proceed as in 2a. Each stripe should be pleated, bound and dyed separately. After completing a stripe, wrap some old cloth round it while working on the next one. This prevents any loose dye from marking the rest of the sample.

Where very fine cloth is being used several stripes can be folded together after the initial creases have been made (110). Pin or tack to keep in place. Then pleat the group of folds as one (111). This needs careful handling as the pleating must be accurate and all the top edges kept level.

Dye each group individually as one stripe.

If the stripes are very close together and must be folded and dyed separately it may be difficult to carry out the zig-zag pleating as there will be insufficient cloth in between each stripe. In this case work in two stages.

1. Pleat and dye alternate stripes (112).

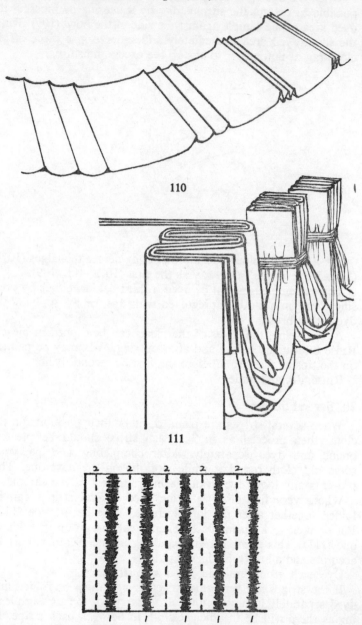

110

111

112

Rinse, dry and untie.

2. Pleat and dye the stripes that were omitted before.

So far the instructions given produce dyed stripes on an undyed background.

To dye the whole sample, apply a solid binding to each bundle of pleats so that the previously dyed area is completely covered. This will reserve the colours dyed on the folded edges. The entire sample can then be immersed in the dyebath and dyed the same or a different colour.

3. FOLDED SQUARES

3a. There are innumerable ways of folding, binding and dyeing a square of cloth, each giving interesting results. The squares may be large or small, but for the first experiments one approximately 8in. x 8in. is a suitable size.

Method

Fold into four, then again diagonally, so that a triangle is formed.

Finally, add binding to the corners or at convenient spots, and dye. Rinse and dry.

Before dyeing a second or third colour, rearrange the bindings. Rinse, dry and untie.

Other examples as :

> 113 A, B, C, D
> 114 A, B, C
> 115 A, B, C
> 116 A, B, C

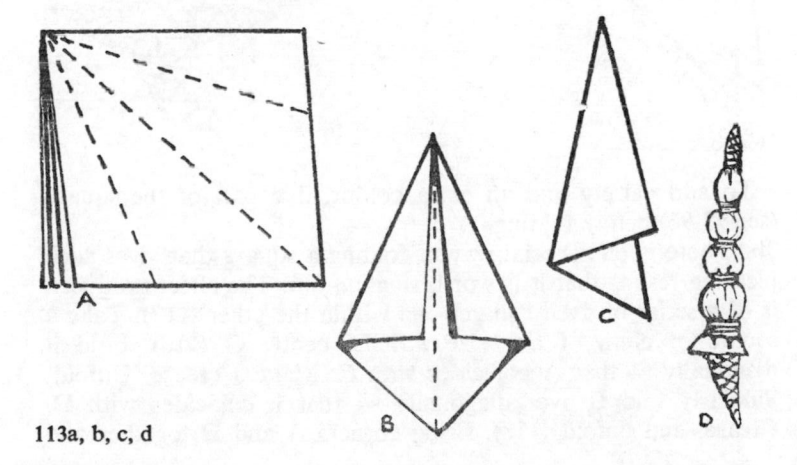

113a, b, c, d

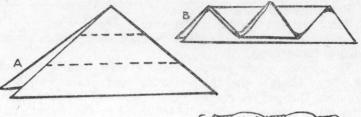

114a b, c

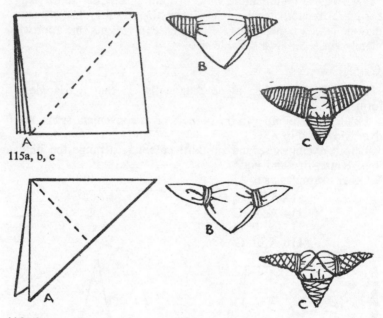

115a, b, c

116a, b, c

To add variety and an extra colour, dye part of the square (see 93-96) before folding.

3b. There is one special way of folding a square that gives such pleasing results that it is worth singling out. The effect produced is of a series of dyed squares one within the other (117). Take a square of cloth of any size ABCD, centre O (118). Fold it diagonally so that A coincides with C. Make a crease. Unfold. Similarly fold B over diagonally so that it coincides with D. Crease, and unfold (118). Bring corners A and D together and

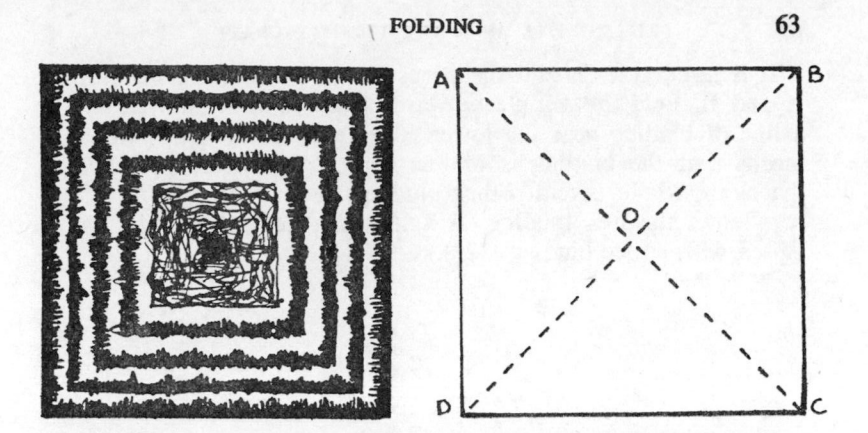

117   118

B to C (119). There is now a triangle which can be called
AOB (120). All the outer edges of the square are along the line
A-B. Mark X midway along AB. Make a series of zig-zag pleats
along AB (121) so that both A and B almost meet at X (122).
The square is now pleated into two columns, one on either side
of OX.

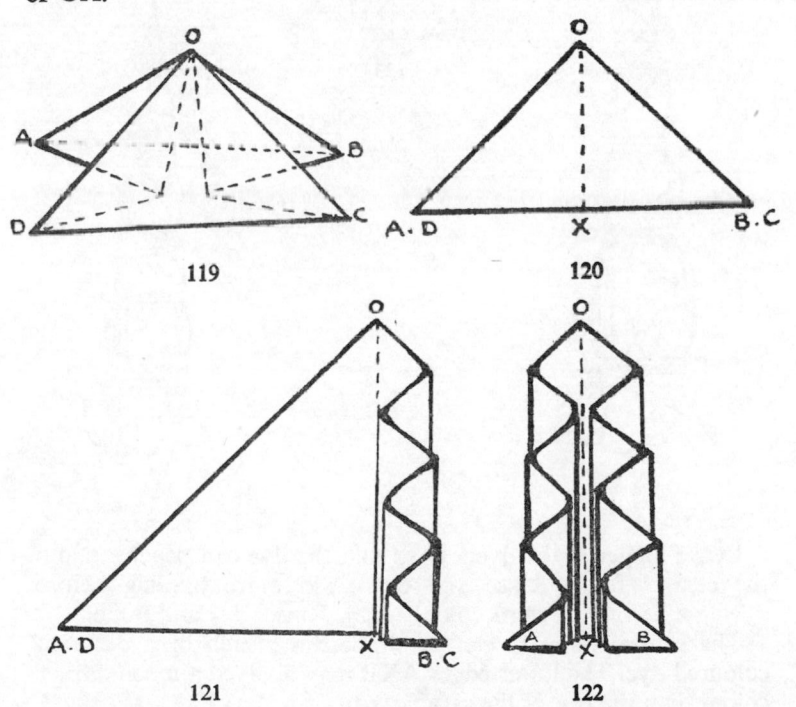

119   120

121   122

It is important that all the edges should be level between A, X and B. Fold the sample outwards from O to X (123). Place a line of binding near the lower edges parallel to AXB, which means that the binding is in line with the grain or weave of the cloth. Make several other bindings farther up towards O, parallel to the first binding. A small area near O may be enclosed with lattice binding (124).

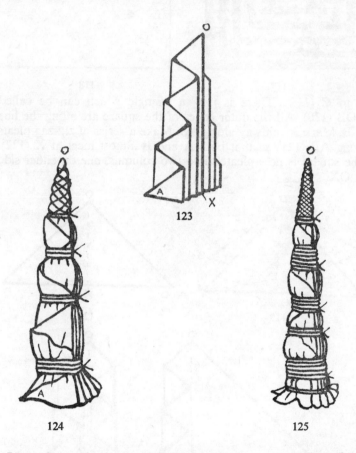

123

124

125

Leave longer in the dyebath so that the dye can penetrate into the central folds. Rinse and dry. Add more binding before dyeing a second or third colour (125). Rinse, dry and untie.

The central point O can be dipped in bleach or a different coloured dye. The lower edges AXB may be dyed a much darker colour than the rest of the sample.

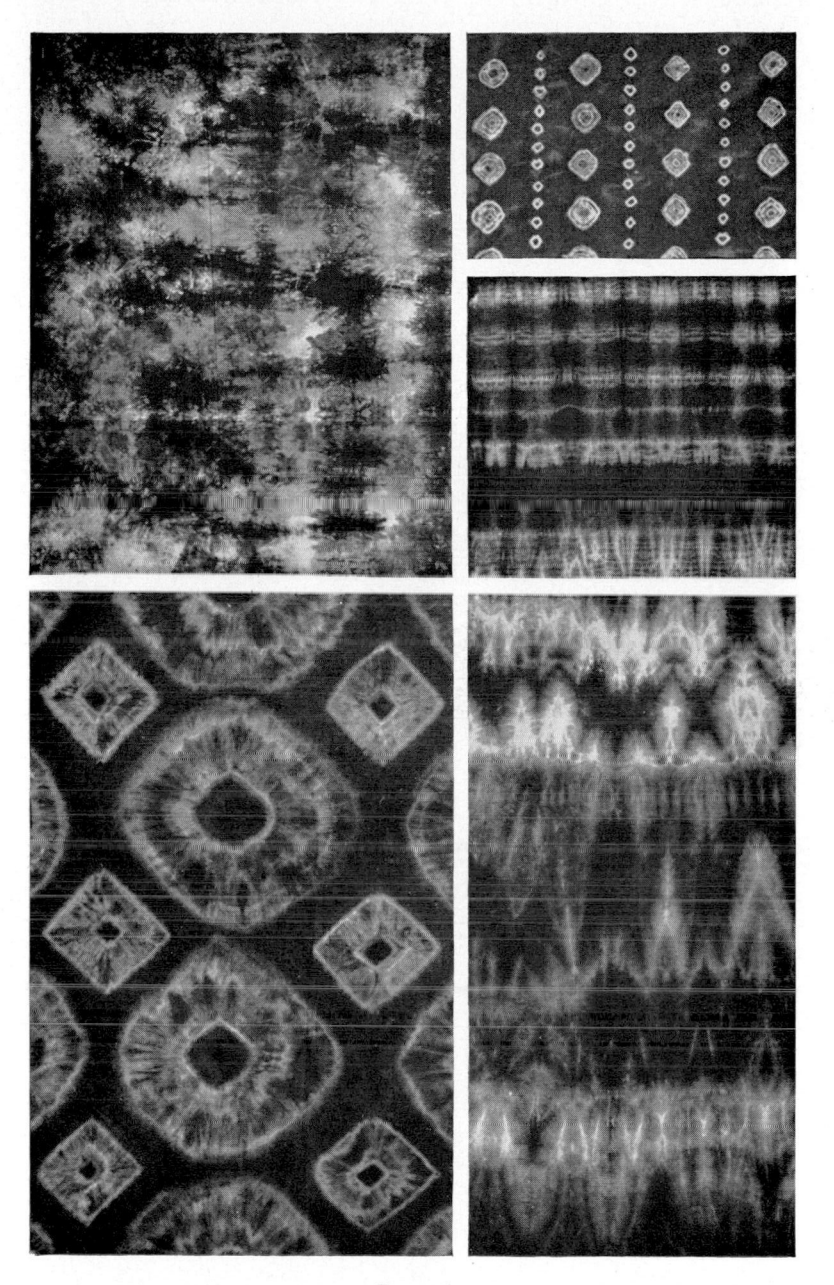

PLATE 1

Top left: *Marbling*
Bottom left: *The knotting technique (round and diamond) used to form an all-over pattern*
Top right: *Alternate rows of small circles and bandhana spots*
Centre right: *Stripes made by binding the cloth*
Bottom right: *Twisting and coiling*

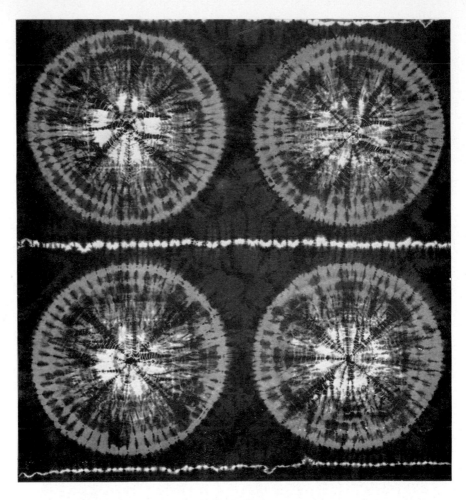

PLATE 2

Length of cloth 1 yard wide. Circles sewn with large tacking stitches and binding added. Background bound to give slight marbled effect. Line is running stitch on single cloth. Part of this design is reproduced on the book jacket

4. ROPE TYING

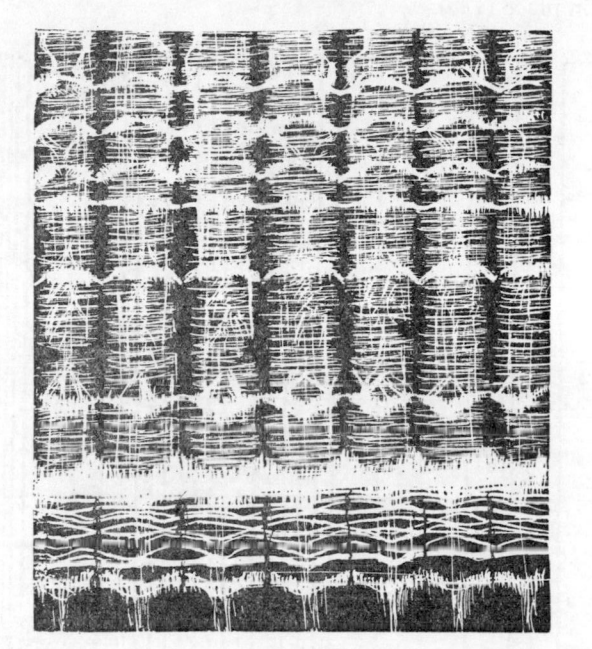

4 (*a*) **Stripes**

This particular style of tie and dye is found in West Africa.
Generally, narrow strips of cloth are used, so that the dye can
penetrate into the closely packed folds. When these strips of
cloth are folded and bound they resemble ropes, hence the name.
Where the cloth is fine, a wider piece can be treated successfully
by this method.

The pattern produced is one of stripes or bands of texture.
Whenever the " rope " is extra bulky allow a longer dyeing time.
If several colours are planned try to arrange the first bindings at
least 1in.-2in. apart to enable the first dyeing to penetrate right
up to the binding even on the inner folds.

Method

Rule a series of parallel lines, following the warp or weft,
approximately one inch apart, or the width of a ruler (126).

Make a crease along each line (127). Fold all the creased
edges together very accurately like accordion pleats. This process is made easier if an iron can be used and a few pins

5—TAD * *

inserted at intervals or a quick loose binding made to hold the
pleats in place (128).

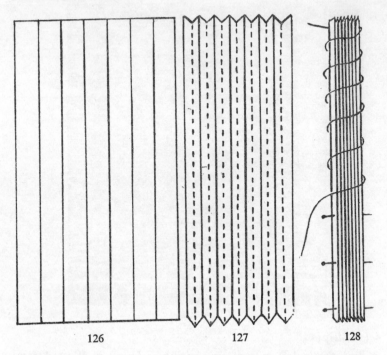

126   127   128

Make blocks or lines of bindings to form the resist stripes
(129). The unbound areas produce the dyed stripes. Lattice binding will give bands of texture. The binding should be made at
right angles to the folded edges of cloth. The stripe produced is
also at right angles to the folded edges or the lines that were
ruled in the first place.

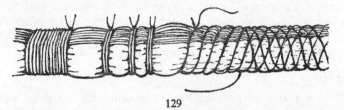

129

Dye, rinse and dry. Make rearrangements to the bindings before dyeing a second or third colour (130, 131).
Rinse, dry and untie.

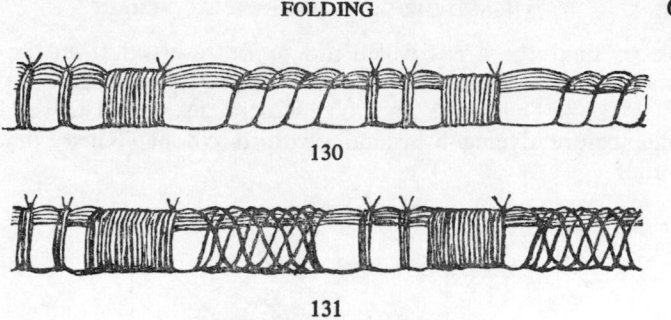

130

131

4 (b) Rope Tying : Diagonal Stripe

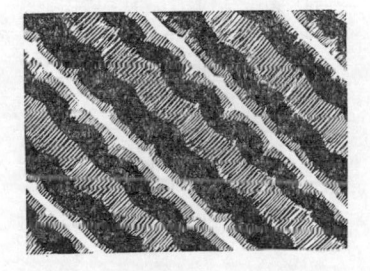

This is a variation of the rope technique, the main difference being the manner in which the material is folded. The pleats are made diagonally across the cloth instead of following the warp or weft as in 4a. The stripes which are produced at right angles to these pleats are therefore dyed diagonally on the sample. Narrow or wide, fine to medium weight material can be used for this method.

Method

Rule parallel lines over the cloth, approximately one inch apart, beginning at corner X (132). If the sample is large, rule the lines farther apart or crease alternate lines for the edges of the accordion pleats.

The angle at which the parallel lines are drawn determines the direction of the finished dyed stripes. For example, lines drawn at an angle of 45 deg. will produce stripes at 45 deg. Lines at an angle of approximately 30 deg. will give finished stripes at an angle of 60 deg. and vice versa.

Make a crease along each line (133), and fold these together (134) until the entire sample is arranged into accordion pleats running diagonally on the sample (135). During this operation it is helpful to use an iron and insert pins to hold the pleats in

place. Bind the areas which are to be reserved from the dye.
Make these bindings at right angles to the folded edges or pencil
lines (136). Dye, rinse and dry. Rearrange or add to the bindings before dyeing a second or third colour. Rinse, dry and
untie.

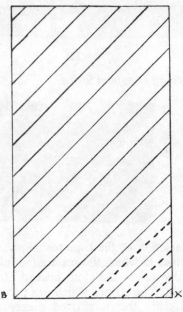

132

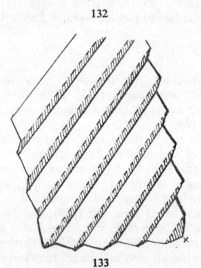

133

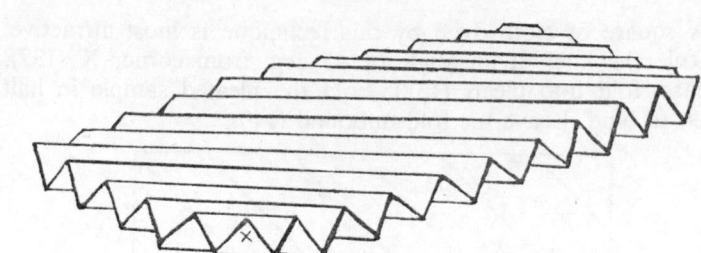

134

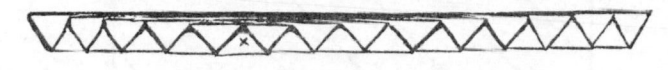

135

136

4 (c) Rope Tying : Trellis Effect

This is a sequel to No. 4b and is carried out in two definite stages.

1. Mark out the sample in diagonal lines, beginning at corner X, crease, fold into accordion pleats, bind, dye, rinse and dry as described in 4b (132-136). Untie and iron out the creases.

2. Stage two is a repetition of the first one except that the parallel lines are ruled from corner B (132) instead of X. This means that they are at right angles to the previous set of lines. Crease and fold into pleats, bind, dye, rinse, dry and untie.

More than one colour can be dyed at each stage if the bindings are adjusted. Both stages can be dyed similarly or in contrasting colours.

To obtain a regular trellis effect both sets of lines should be ruled at the same angle and at the same distance apart.

A square of cloth dyed by this technique is most attractive.
Rule the lines at an angle of 45 deg. from corner X (137).
Crease, fold into pleats (138). Fold the pleated sample in half
(139) to bind. Leave the fold unbound (140).

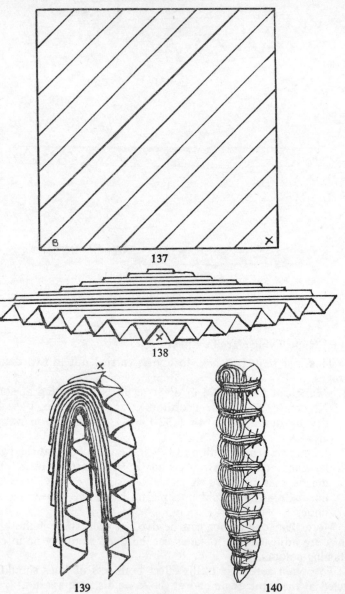

137

138

139   140

Dye as required. Rinse, dry, untie and iron.

If a trellis effect is desired, repeat the whole process, beginning at corner B.

4 (d) Zig-zag Stripe : Rope Technique

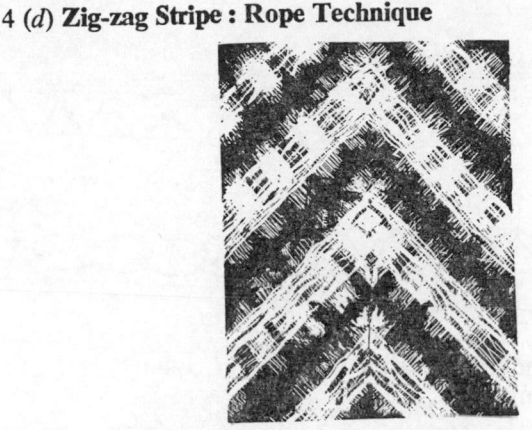

This is another development of the diagonal rope technique, the main difference being that the cloth is folded lengthwise before the parallel lines are ruled.

Although size is no obstacle the coarser grained cloths are unsuitable.

Method

A single zig-zag (141)S

Fold the material in half lengthwise (142)S. Pin or tack the selvedges together.

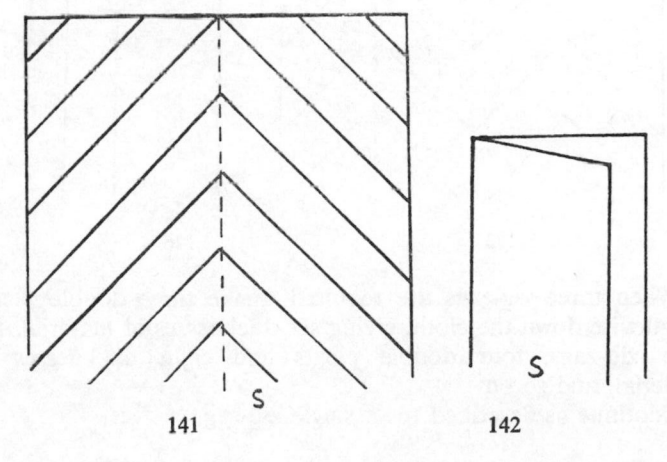

141   142

Work on the double cloth as if it were single. Mark parallel diagonal lines from one corner and crease them. Fold into accordion pleats (143), bind (144), dye, rinse and dry as described for diagonal stripe 4b.

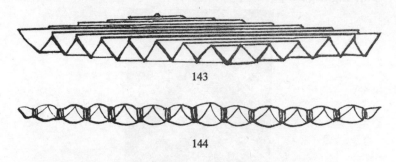

143

144

Add further bindings for a second or third colour.
Rinse, dry and untie.

Several zig-zags

If two zig-zags are required (145)D, fold cloth in half lengthways, then turn each selvedge edge back to the centre fold, giving four thicknesses of material (146)D. From this point work in exactly the same manner as for the single zig-zag (143, 144, 147).

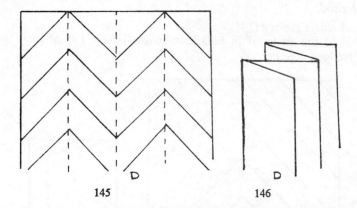

145   146

When three zig-zags are required, make three double pleats lengthwise down the cloth, giving six thicknesses of material, for four zig-zags, four double pleats and eight thicknesses of material, and so on.

Continue as described for a single zig-zag.

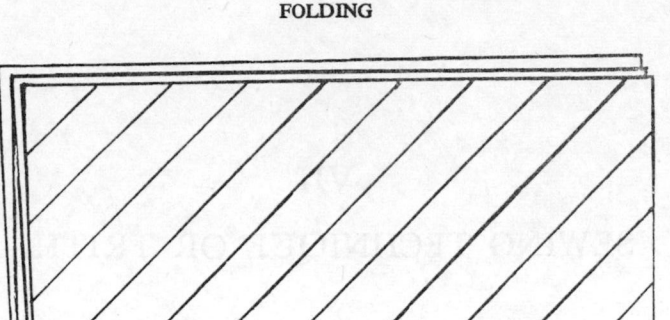

147

Folding the cloth lengthwise produces zig-zags running across the fabric. If the first folds are made across the sample, the zig-zag stripe will be dyed lengthwise on the cloth (147).

To cut down the binding in any of the diagonal stripe techniques, especially where there is a long thin sample, work as follows:

Bind a small area in the centre of the "rope" singly, then bring the two ends together and bind as one unit (as in 140).

VII

SEWING TECHNIQUE OR TRITIK

IN most tie-and-dye countries the sewing or tritik method has been used. In West Africa today, sewing methods, with fine strands of raffia as the sewing thread, are widely practised.

The success of the sewing method is entirely dependent on the ability to draw up the material into gathers so closely on the sewing thread that the dye cannot penetrate into the folds. It is essential therefore to have very strong thread that does not break half-way through the operation, and that will remain taut, while supporting the weight of the closely gathered cloth, during the process of dyeing.

Linen carpet thread (No. 18 and No. 25) is very suitable for this purpose, used single, or double where extra strength is needed. Crewel needles (sizes 3-7) are better than ordinary sewing needles, as they accommodate the thick thread without undue bulk, and thus avoid making permanent holes in the fabric.

Medium to fine weave fabrics are best.

There is one rule that applies to all sewing methods: *Always make a large knot in the thread before beginning to sew and a large knot in the thread as soon as it is taken out of the needle or cut.* This means there is a large knot at either end of a line of sewing.

Never leave a loose end of thread anywhere without a knot.

If the lines of sewing stretch right across the material, keep all the knots at the edges.

When the pattern is small, single thread is sufficient, but double thread is essential where there is a large area to be sewn, for instance where a line of sewing extends right across the cloth. If a thread is not strong enough it will snap during the pulling up and the pattern will be spoilt, or lost completely.

For the pulling up process gradually slide the cloth along each sewing thread until it is bunched into a solid mass of gathers at one end. Make sure that the knot at the end of the thread is bulky enough to hold the cloth in position. The gathered cloth will slip off the thread if the knot does not form an adequate barrier.

If the tightening up process has been carried out properly the sewing thread should not be visible. The exceptions are when oversewing a bulky hem or where a double row of oversewing is being used.

After pulling up the thread tightly the ultimate success of the pattern depends on a firm secure fastening off, that will not slacken in the slightest while the sample is dyed. It must be able to keep the closely packed folds of cloth from bursting away from the thread.

FASTENING-OFF METHODS

The following suggestions should cover any eventuality. There is no " one " way of fastening off after sewing ; different problems require different solutions.

Tying

As in binding, where there are two ends adjoining one another, the best way of fastening off after pulling up the threads is to tie those ends together.

Back Stitch

After all the sewing has been completed and the double or single thread has been tightened up to its limit, several back-stitches can be used for fastening off. The difficulty with this method is to prevent the thread from slipping while the back-stitches are being sewn. To mitigate this danger, grip the bunched-up cloth, at the same time pressing the left thumb securely on the spot where the thread emerges from the last fold of cloth. Sew the backstitches firmly so that no further loosening of the thread is possible.

Making a False End for Tying

If, after sewing, a solitary end of thread needs fastening off (148) and backstitching is impracticable, it is quite easy to create a false end for tying to it.

Method

Thread a needle with a small fresh length of thread and make a substantial knot at one end. With one or more slip stitches, attach the new thread to the cloth adjacent to the existing end (149). The odd end can now be tied up with the new end (150).

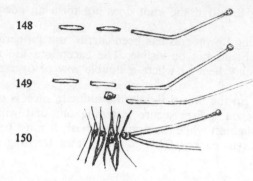

A Join

This method is also used for attaching an additional sewing thread if the first one is not quite long enough to finish a line of sewing (151, 152). Knot the end of the first thread X. Overlap the new thread for two or three stitches, then continue the line of sewing (152a and b).

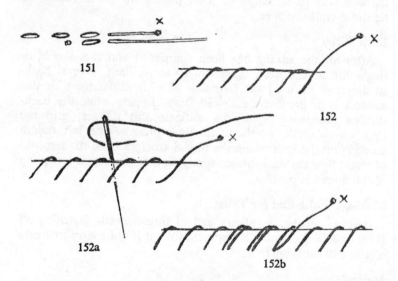

Cutting the Sewing Thread to Fasten Off

In some instances, more especially with oversewing where a long line of sewing is involved, it is better to make the fastening off in the middle of the row, or even to make several breaks where there is an exceptionally lengthy line of sewing.

Method

153 ///

154 /////////////////////////////

Check up to see that the line of sewing has a solid knot at each end. Ease the sewing thread into a loop in the centre of the row, or at any other spot chosen to make a break for fastening off (153). Cut the thread and knot the two ends thus formed. Pull up both pieces of thread (154), bunching the cloth as tightly as possible. Tie the two ends into a single knot, then pull the two threads away from each other until the gap in the line of sewing closes right up. Tie the ends together again until it is impossible for the threads to slacken.

Separating a Double Thread

When a double thread is used for sewing (155) and there is no other means of fastening off, it is possible to tie the two strands into a knot.

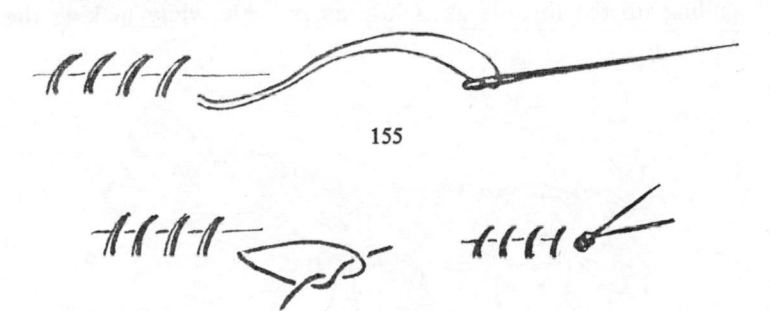

155

156   157

Method

Complete the row of sewing and pull up the thread until the cloth is bunched into a compact mass. Cut the thread three or

four inches beyond the cloth. Separate the two strands and tie
them into a single knot (156). Pull the two strands in opposite
directions, and give a final tug to tighten the row of sewing before completing the knot (157). If this stage can be manœuvred
while the left thumb is pressed on the first half of the knot to
prevent it from slipping a very much more effective fastening off
will be achieved. After the knot has been tied twice it is advisable to tie it again several times to build up a knot big enough
to keep the cloth from slipping off the thread.

Tying Both Ends of a Line of Sewing Together

After completing a row of running or oversewing stitches
right across a sample, it is often more advantageous to tie both
ends of the one row together for a satisfactory fastening off
(158). This prevents the edges of the sample from curling in-
wards and thus missing the dye. It makes a neat convenient roll
for dyeing and quite often produces more clearly defined resist
areas. This method of fastening off can *only* be used on samples
where lines or bands of sewing stretch across from one side of
the cloth to the other.

Method

Check up that both ends of all the sewing threads are knotted.
Pull up these threads so that the cloth is bunched up closely
in the centre. With the right side of the sample outside, turn
back the left edge to meet the right edge of the cloth as if making
a roll or tube. Tie both ends of each line of sewing together,
pulling up the threads as tightly as possible while making the
knot.

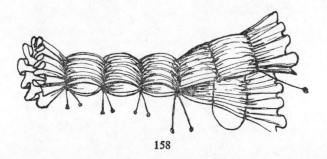

158

Fastening Off a Continuous Sewing Thread

When several lines of sewing have been made on one continuous thread (159) this can be tightened and fastened off by any of the methods described on p. 75.

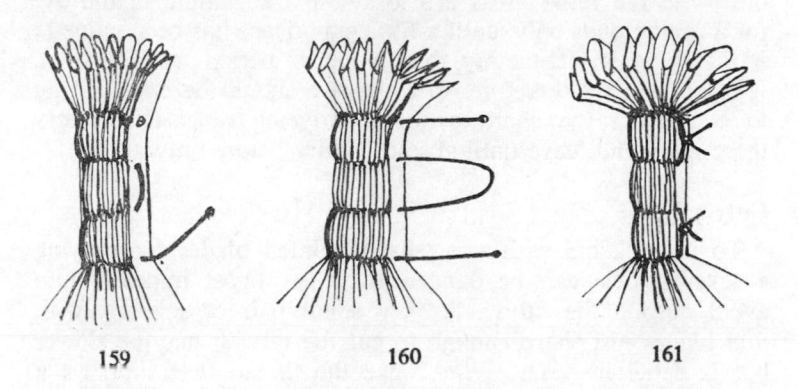

159   160   161

If it is necessary to fasten off each row separately proceed as follows. Pull out the loops at both sides of the sample where the thread is carried from one row to the next. Cut each loop and knot the ends. Then tie both ends of each row of sewing together to form a tube (158).

The loops can be pulled out on one side only (160), cut, the ends knotted, then tied together in pairs (161).

In both cases the cloth must be bunched up as tightly as possible before the thread is tied finally.

GENERAL HINTS ON SEWING METHODS

The following points apply to all sewing methods :

Sewing

The texture or treatment of the design may be varied by using small or large stitches as well as coarser and finer thread.

Finish all the sewing on a small sample before beginning to pull up the threads ; it is much more difficult to work on a partially gathered piece of cloth than one that is flat. With a larger sample the threads can be tightened a little at one end if economy in the use of thread is being considered. Allow a generous gap between the area that is being sewn and that which is bunched up. There should be enough ungathered cloth left to enable the rest of the sewing to be carried out comfortably.

Dyeing

The sewing technique is usually classed as shallow or thin tying and therefore requires a shorter time in the dyebath, otherwise the resist areas are lost. Dip the sample in the dye for a few seconds only, until a little experience has been gained ; if the resist is satisfactory then a longer period may be tried. It is imperative, therefore, that the dye should be extra strong to counteract the shortness of the dyeing time. Rinse very thoroughly and leave until absolutely dry before untying.

Untying

To use scissors with very sharp pointed blades for untying a sewn sample can be dangerous. It is almost impossible to avoid cutting the fabric. A very small pair of scissors, with thin blades just sharp enough to cut the thread, may be slower but is definitely safer. When once the thread that supports a row of sewing is cut, the cloth usually frees itself without further trouble.

The two most obvious places to cut a sewing thread are :

1. At every knot. Give the knot a slight pull so that the blades of the scissors can slide underneath to snip it off, making sure there is no fabric being snipped at the same time.

2. At any point where two threads are tied together. Insert the blade of the scissors into the small triangle that is formed after pulling the knotted thread away from the cloth, and cut both sides of the knot (46).

Sometimes it is necessary to cut the thread in the centre of a row of sewing. This requires great care and precision. Part the folds of cloth until the thread is visible. Either insert the tip of a pair of scissors and snip the thread, or better still, lever the blunt end of a needle under the small piece of taut thread, until there is enough room to insert the blade of the scissors to cut it.

The thread used in oversewing can be cut in several places— at each knot, and along the centre of the row.

There are three distinct classes in the sewing technique:

1. Running or Tacking Stitches on Single Cloth.
2. Running or Tacking Stitches on Double Cloth or Folded Cloth.
3. Oversewing or Whipping Stitch.

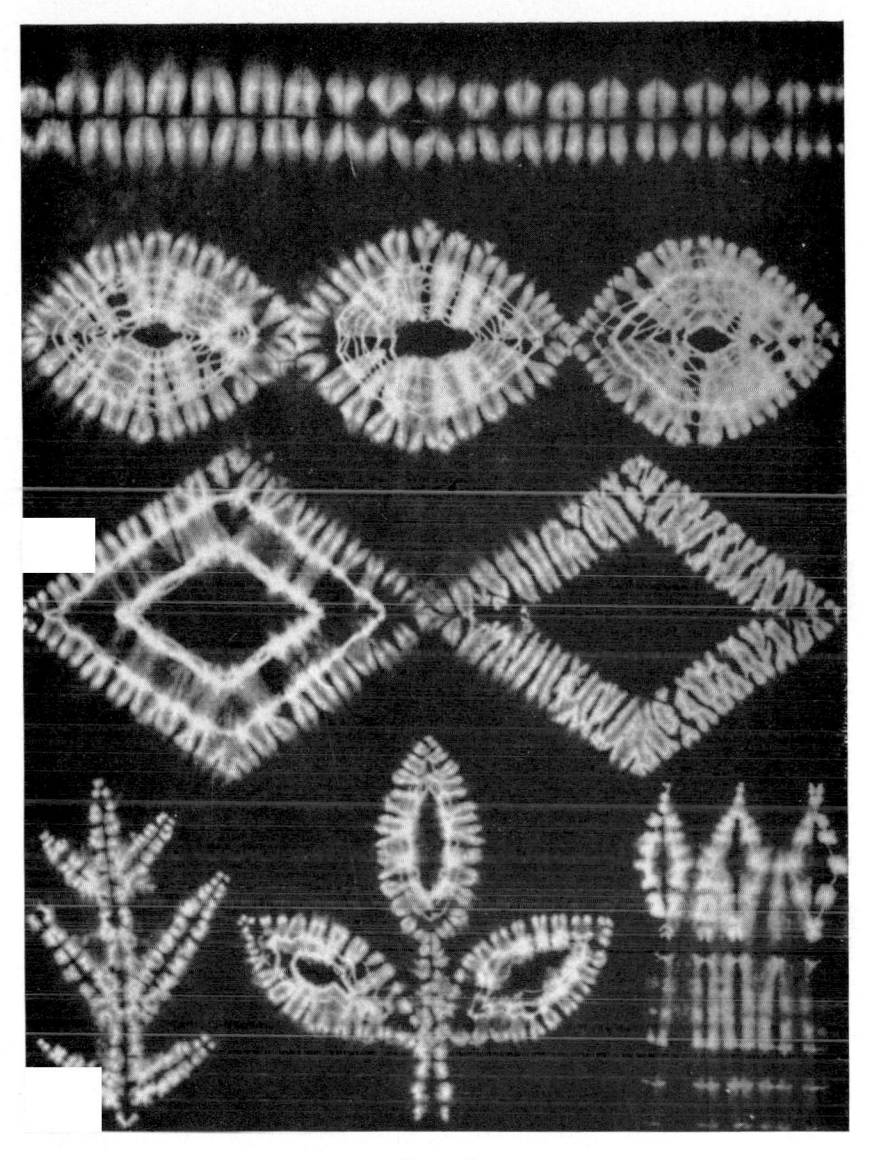

PLATE 3

Panel, approx. 12 × 18 in. Sampler showing effects achieved by the method of running stitch on double cloth

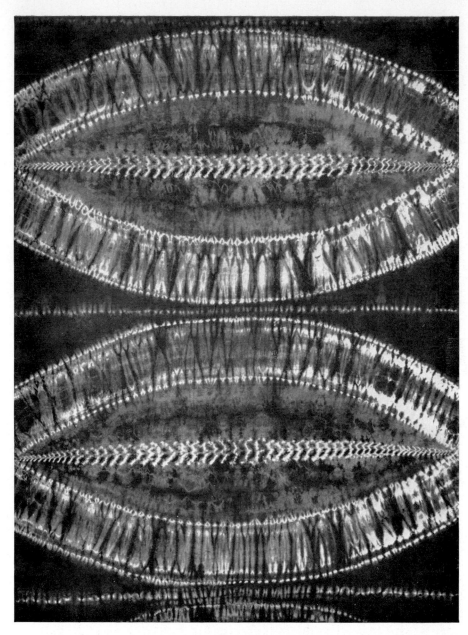

PLATE 4

Length of cloth 1 yard wide. Ruched ovals obtained by tucking. Centre of each oval is oversewn and dyed separately

1. RUNNING OR TACKING STITCHES ON SINGLE CLOTH

1 (a) **Lines and Bands**

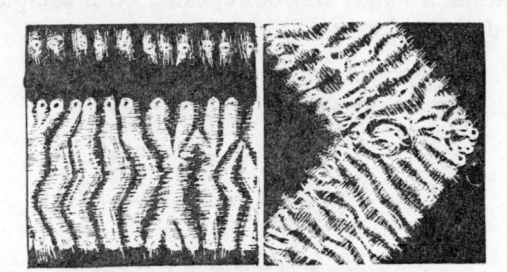

Left, above: *Single line of running stitches*
Below: *Several lines forming a band of texture*
Right: *Zig-zag band of texture*

Method

Mark the cloth with a crease or a pencil line in the direction of the row of sewing. Make a large knot in the thread. Sew along the line (162), cut off the thread and make a knot at the end (163a). Long and shorter stitches may be combined to vary the texture (163c). Long stitches create a better resist.

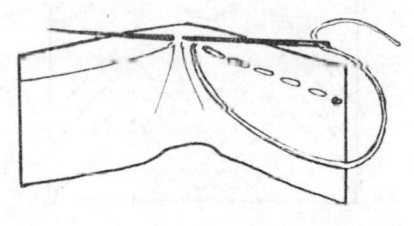

162

Pull up the thread so that the cloth is collected into a tight mass of gathers (164) and fasten off by tying two ends together where possible (165). This must be done really effectively or there will be no resist produced. Sewing on single cloth is the shallowest tying method and should be given a very short dip in the dyebath. Wet-out sample before dyeing.

Rinse thoroughly, dry and untie.

Several parallel lines of sewing, placed approximately $\frac{1}{4} - \frac{1}{2}$ inch apart, make a pleasing "band" of texture (163b). The thread can be carried on from one line to the next and the " band " drawn up as one line of sewing (159).

Dye as above.

These lines and bands can be repeated on a sample to form an all-over design (163b and c).

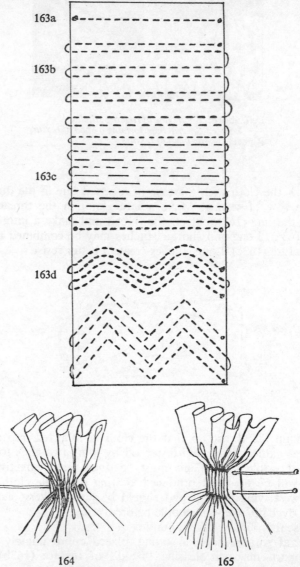

163a

163b

163c

163d

164   165

Where two or more colours are being dyed, some of the lines of sewing can be left slack until after the first dyeing. They can then be tightened and fastened off before dyeing the next colour.

1 (b) Wavy, Curved or Zig-Zag Bands, etc.

These " bands " of running stitches need not necessarily be straight but can change direction, forming curves or zig-zags, etc. (163d).

Method

Mark out the design on the cloth indicating where each line of stitches is to be placed. To make the outline of the bands more definite, use small to medium stitches for the outside, but to save time larger stitches are permissible for the filling-in rows. Use double thread when there is likely to be any strain. The whole block can be sewn on the one piece of thread, drawn up, and secured with one fastening off. Dye in one or more colours as 1 (a).

1 (c) An All-Over Sewn Texture

Lines of running stitches repeated over an area of cloth will give a texture that resembles smocking. If a large area of this texture is planned the sewing up stage can become very tedious. Larger stitches will save time, or rather, a mixture of large and small stitches along each row (163c). Keep all the knots at the side, or use a very long length of double thread which will extend over a considerable area. This can be drawn up so that one fastening off is made (159), or the cloth may be formed into a tube for the fastening off (158).

Leave some of the rows slack until after the first or second colour has been dyed. Binding can also be added to the tube of gathered-up cloth, after the first dyeing, to give stripes (166).

166

A darker dye can be brushed on the tightly packed folds after the first or second dyeing.

To speed up the sewing process on a long length of cloth, fold the entire sample in half, across or lengthways, and sew on the double cloth. Keep the sample flat for dyeing (161).

1 (d) A Resist Line

A narrow resist line between two given points, either straight or curved, can be formed on the cloth by the running stitch technique.

Method

Draw the required line AB (167).

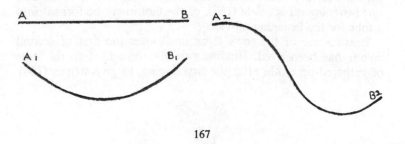

167

Take a needle with strong thread, knotted at one end, and sew from B — A, using medium stitches (168). Take the needle back and insert it in the cloth just beyond B (169). Pass the needle underneath the line, bringing it to the surface again just beyond A. A loop of thread now encircles the sewn line (170).

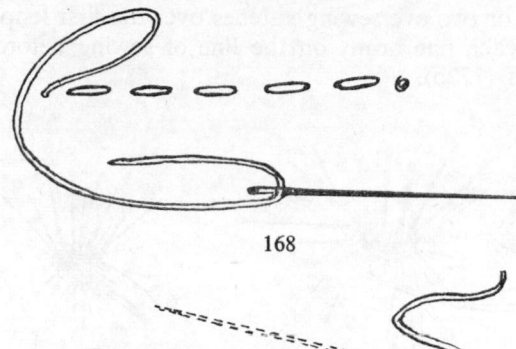

168

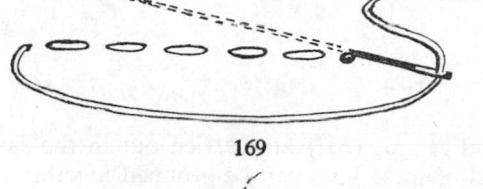

169

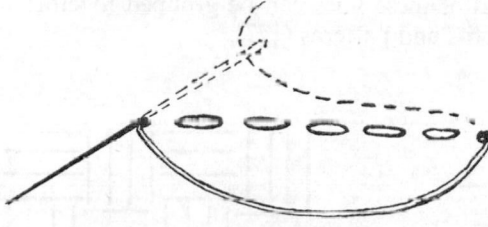

170

Pull out the knotted end at B for about 2 inches. Tighten the sewing thread at A so that the line of sewing is gathered up into a compact bunch with the loop covering any of the original pencil line that happens to be showing (171). This is very important, especially with curves, as it ensures that the correct direction of the line is maintained. Tie both ends of the thread together so that the loop grips the line of sewing absolutely firm and taut. If a more pronounced resist is aimed

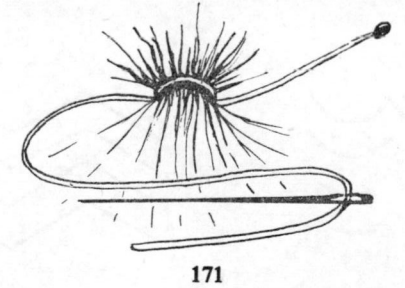

171

at take one or two oversewing stitches over the first loop (172a), pulling up each one firmly on the line of sewing before finally fastening off (172b).

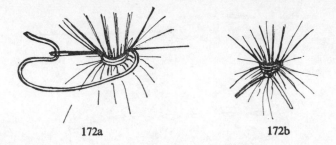

172a   172b

A_1, B_1 and A_2, B_2 (167) are carried out in the same way as A B. Several of these lines can be grouped together to form interesting motifs and patterns (173).

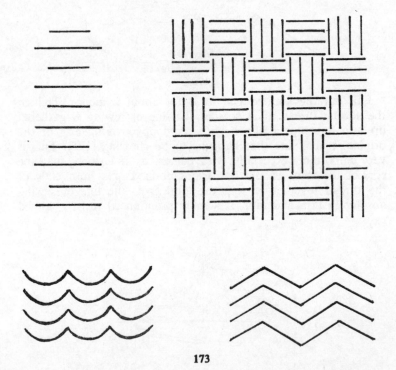

173

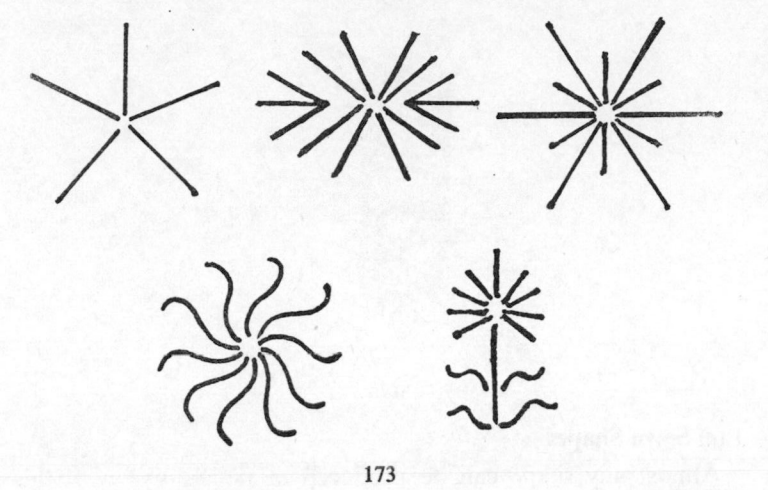

173

After completing the resist straight line it is possible to make a block of texture by adding a double layer of oversewing stitches down the cloth, beyond, and in line with A B. This can be done before or after the first dyeing (174a, b and c).

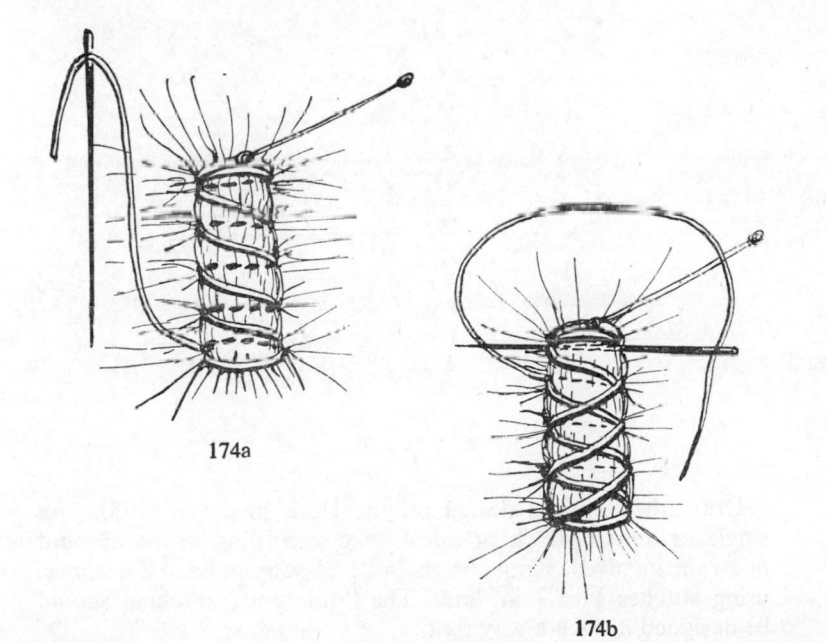

174a

174b

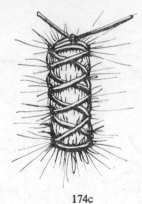

174c

1 (*e*) Sewn Shapes

Almost any shape can be produced in tie-and-dye with this sewing method. The principle of using a running stitch outline, filled in with rows of stitching, can be applied to very simple or quite complicated shapes.

Method

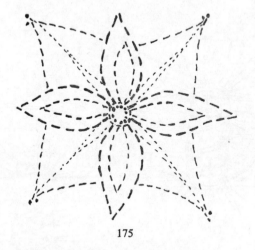

175

Draw the required design on the cloth in pencil (175). Use single or double, thick or fine thread according to the amount of strain involved. Knot the thread and sew round the outlines, using stitches $\frac{1}{8}$ to $\frac{1}{2}$ in. long. The " filling-in " stitching should be designed in such a way that :

(a) the rows are parallel to each other.

(b) the rows are parallel to the outline as far as possible (176).

(c) the rows help to express the form of the object being depicted.

For instance, a leaf shape could have the filling-in lines of sewing placed to represent veins (177b).

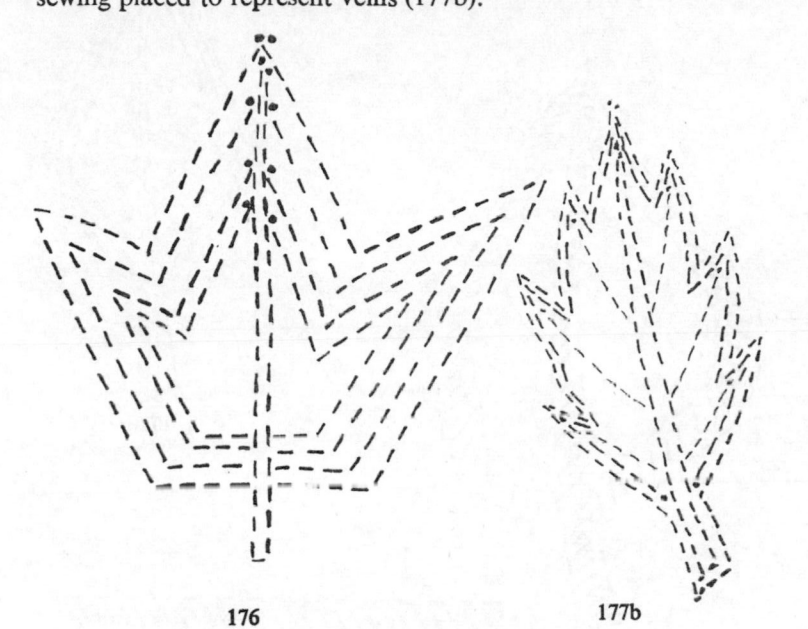

176   177b

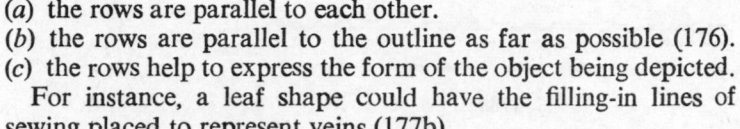

177a

Complete all the sewing on the design before pulling up the threads and fastening off.

Some of the threads may be left slack until after the first or second dyeing. If a definite sequence of pulling up has been planned beforehand it is helpful if the sewing is carried out in different coloured threads. For example :

White threads for the areas to be drawn up *before* the first dyeing.

Fawn thread for the parts to be drawn up before the second dyeing.

Brown or black threads for those rows to be left for the last dyeing, etc.

It is possible to use previously dyed threads for the sewing technique.

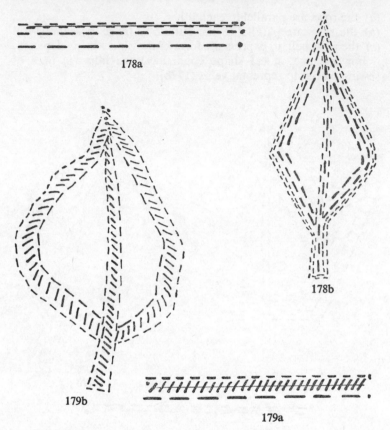

178a

178b

179b

179a

Dye for a short time, rinse and dry thoroughly before untying.

To add importance and emphasis to the outline of a shape composed of running stitches on single cloth, with or without a central area of texture, 2, 3 or 4 lines may be sewn as in (177a and b) and (178a and b). (179a and b) include oversewing.

In every case sew the row of stitches nearest to the pencil line first of all, to preserve a good contour. The other lines need not follow the pencil line so accurately.

The thickness of the threads for the various rows may be varied, the inner rows of double or single cotton or finer thread.

This method of outlining can be made most expressive and the great advantage is that the pulling up and untying processes are easier than for the oversewing method.

1 (f) Sewn Spirals

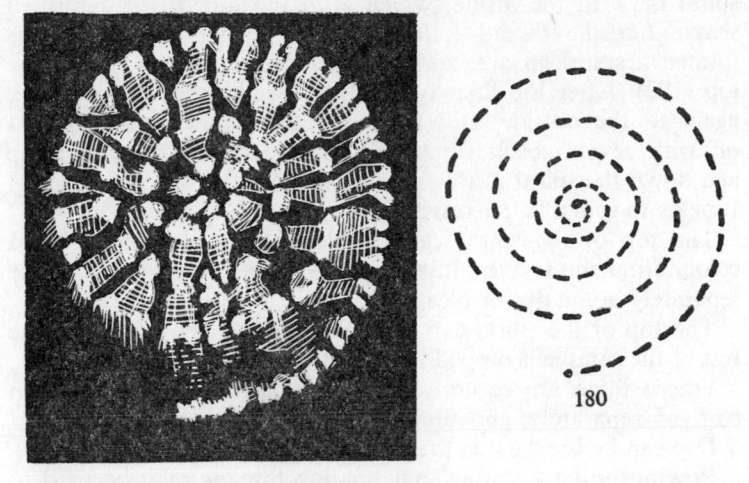

180

Method

Draw the required shape on the cloth in pencil. Use single thread for a small spiral but double for a medium to large spiral. Make an extra large knot in the thread. Beginning at the centre, sew along the pencil line until the outer edge of the spiral is reached (180). Draw up the thread from the needle end or from both ends. This is when the large knot in the centre is an advantage. Tighten the thread until the cloth is packed into a solid mass of gathers. The spiral has now taken on the shape of a snail's shell (181). Fasten off both ends of the thread

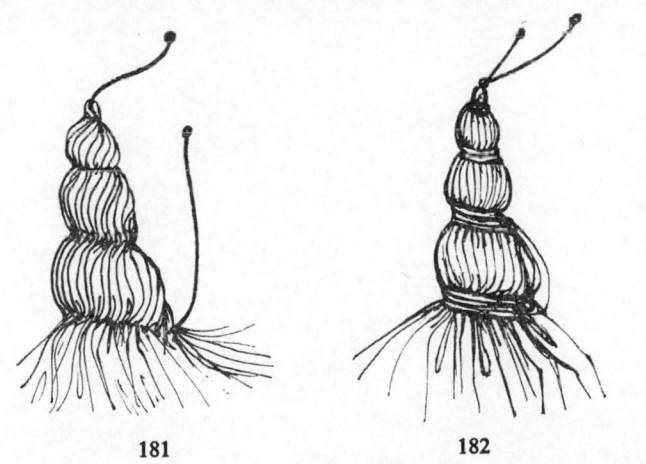

181   182

separately, or wind the thread from the outer edge of the
spiral back to the inside, which is at the top of the snailshell
shape. Let the thread follow the line of sewing, which has
formed a spiral groove, and tie it to the knotted thread at the
top (182). After the first dyeing the thread can be taken back
again to the outside, still following the groove, and fastened
off with several back stitches. The thread can be wound up
and down the spiral in this manner again, after the next dyeing.
It helps to give a better resist.

The top of the spiral can be bleached or dyed a different
colour from the rest, by inverting the tip of the snailshell shape
separately in the dye or bleach.

The top of the spiral can be withheld from the dye while the
rest of the sample is dipped in a second colour.

Where there are several spirals on a sample, each one can
be dyed separately, and thus differently from the others.

Dye can be brushed on the outside folds.

Previously dyed sewing and binding threads may be used.

The spiral method may be adapted to other shapes, for
instance, the square, rectangle (183), triangle (184) and to many

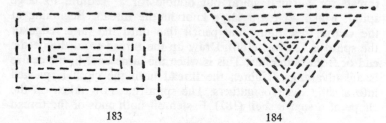

183   184

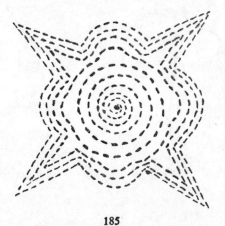

185

irregular shaped figures. The outer rows of a spiral shape can be gradually extended into scallops, petal shapes or 'V' shapes (185).

2. SEWING ON FOLDED OR DOUBLE CLOTH

Anyone wishing to tackle the craft of tie-dyeing seriously, or desiring to create a wide range of designs, would be well advised to spend some time mastering this particular technique. In most cases, the simplest form of stitching is sufficient to give good results. The most essential factor is the ability to pull up the sewing thread tightly and fasten off securely. The fact that sewing must be used for this technique need not deter those who have little or no skill with the needle, as ingenuity in arranging shapes and planning the colour combinations is more important for arriving at successful designs. Very small or really large-scale patterns are possible with this method, which is often combined with suitable binding.

People in most tie-and-dye areas of the world have made full use of this effective way of obtaining resist shapes.

The choice of thread depends on :

(a) Kind of cloth—fine thread for fine or medium cloths ; thicker cloths need stronger thread.

(b) Size of pattern. Fine cotton or Sylko used double is suitable for some very tiny designs, the larger patterns need stronger thread, single or double.

(c) Length of each particular line of sewing. A very short line needs single thread ; a long line double thread.

The technique of sewing on double cloth can be divided into two main sections, each one equally important and both permitting innumerable variations.

2 (a) Lines and Stripes

These can be made in any direction on the cloth and may be straight, curved or zig-zag.

Method

Rule a line for the centre of each stripe and fold the cloth over double along it. Make a row of running or tacking stitches on double cloth just below the fold (186) beginning and ending with a large knot. Where there are several rows of sewing on one stripe or where a group of lines or stripes are close enough together, use a continuous sewing thread (187). Complete all the sewing on the sample, draw up the threads very tightly

and fasten off (188) securely. Immerse the sample in the dye
for a few seconds to begin with; if the resist is satisfactory,
increase the dyeing time. Some of the threads can be left slack
until after the first dyeing. These can then be drawn up before
the second or third dyeing. After the final dyeing rinse
thoroughly, dry and untie.

Several lines or stripes can be folded together and sewn as
one (189).

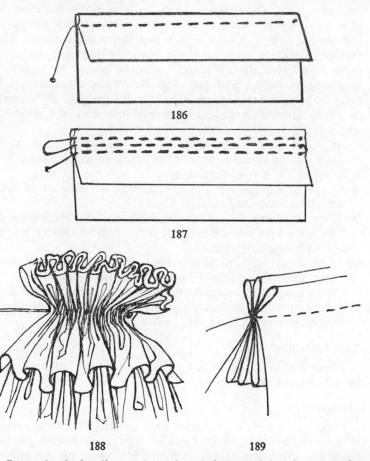

186

187

188   189

Instead of the lines of sewing being straight they can be
sewn in curved and zig-zag bands as in 190. Fold the cloth
over double, mark the direction of the rows of sewing. Complete
all the sewing, using medium stitches on the outside but larger

ones for the filling-in rows. Pull up the threads, fasten off and
dye as planned.

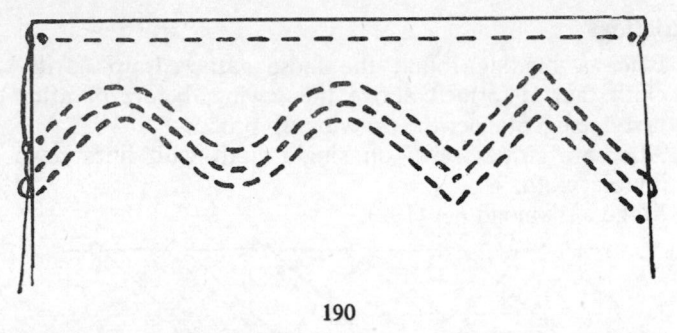

190

2 (*b*) Curved and Zig-zag Tucks

Method

Mark the direction of the tucks in pencil on the cloth. Crease
along the lines and sew on the double cloth to form a narrow
tuck (191a and b). The fabric will need easing in round the
curves and a small pleat will have to be made at the back
of each point on the zig-zags. More than one line of sewing
may be made.

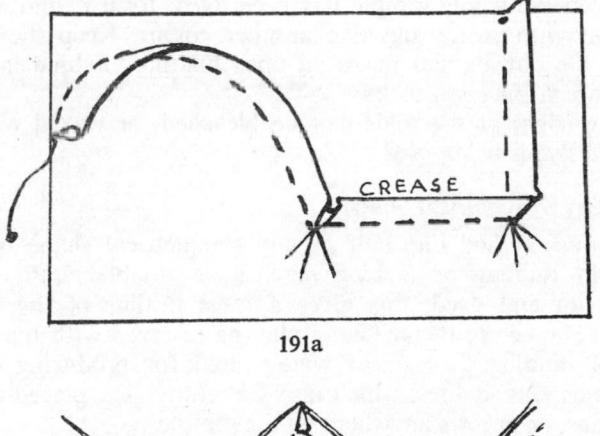

191a

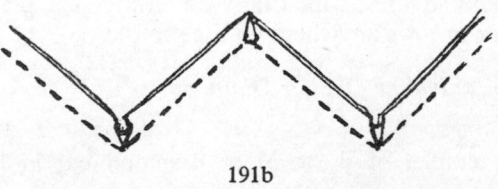

191b

Pull up the threads after completing the sewing and fasten off. Dye, rinse and untie.

Variations

1. Place a binding round the loose gathered up "frill" of cloth that is formed above the sewing, before or after the first dyeing. Stagger the drawing-up process.
2. Alternate stripes sewn on single cloth with lines sewn on double cloth.
3. Make a diamond net (192).

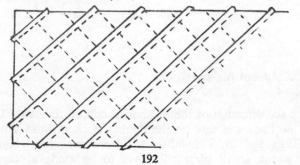

192

4. Paint dye on the tips of the fold after the whole sample has been dyed. This should be in a darker or contrasting colour from the main one.
5. When the whole sample has been dyed, form it into a coil, bind with string and dye another colour. Keep the tucks on the outside and make an open binding, or bind in lines between the sewn tucks.
6. The edges of the folds can be bleached, or waxed when a cold dye is being used.

2 (c) Any Symmetrical Shape

By this method one half of any symmetrical shape is outlined in running or tacking stitches on double cloth. When drawn up and dyed, this gives a resist outline of the whole shape. The centre of the shape may be reserved with the addition of binding. It is most widely used for producing ovals, diamonds and squares, which may be of any size, placed alone, in groups, or in rows anywhere on the sample.

2 (c) (i) An Individual Oval or Diamond
Method

Make a templet of the oval or diamond cut in half (193).

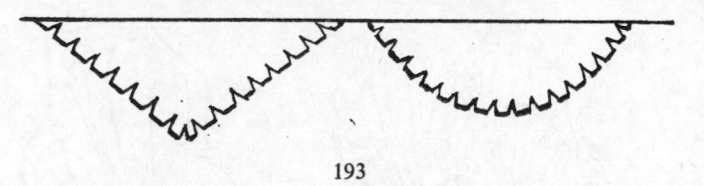

193

Draw a pencil line for the centre of the shape and fold the cloth over double along it. Place the straight edge of the templet to the edge of the fold, at the required spot. Draw round it in pencil (194). Keep the material in place with a few pins; these are more necessary when working on a large-scale pattern. Sew from right to left along the pencil outline, beginning and ending at the folded edge (195).

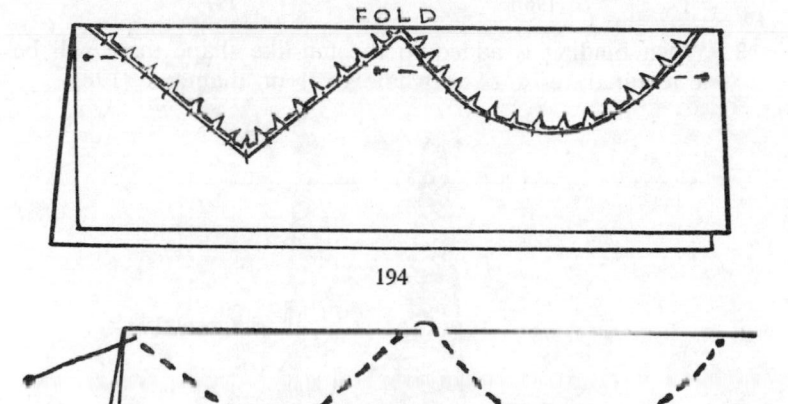

194

195

Two or three parallel rows of stitching can be made inside the shape, to give it a bold outline. Cut and knot the thread. Pull it up very tightly (196) and tie both ends together. The curved outline is now flattened, and the former straight folded edge is frilled into a small fan-like shape projecting above the line of sewing.

A little binding may be added along the line of sewing of each shape (197).

1. If the sample is dyed at this stage there will be a resist outline.

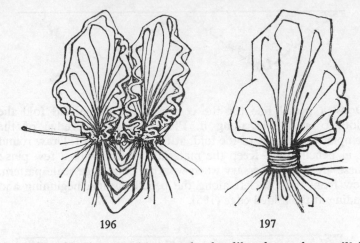

196   197

2. When binding is added to the fan-like shape there will be a textured resist of a whole oval or diamond (198).

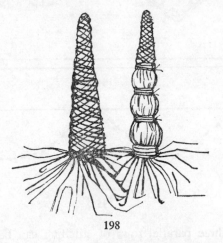

198

3. The small fan can be dyed separately by inverting it in the dye. This gives a coloured diamond or oval on an undyed ground.
4. After the sample has been dyed as No. 1, 2 or 3, the fan shape can be covered with close binding and the whole sample dyed a second colour. This gives an oval or diamond on a different coloured background.
5. The whole sample can be dyed, then the fan shape dipped in bleach. Binding may be added for this.

6. After dyeing the sample, the tips of the bound shape may have another coloured dye brushed on. Wax may be applied to it before a second colour is dyed.

2 (c) (ii) A Row of Ovals or Diamonds

The oval and diamond shape just described may be repeated to form a row, across or down a length of cloth. The shapes may be very large or small, similar or dissimilar. The rows may be repeated to form an all-over pattern.

Method

Rule a line to indicate the centre of the row of shapes. Fold the cloth over double along this line and pin or tack to keep it in place.

Make a templet, of the required oval or diamond cut in half (193). Place the straight edge of the templet to the folded edge of the cloth. Draw round it lightly in pencil (194). Move the templet further along the fold so that it just touches the shape already drawn. Mark the next outline in pencil (194). Continue in this way to the end of the row.

It is possible when making the templet to snip out small " V's " along the outside edge to indicate the position of the stitches (193). Mark these with a dot on the cloth. This helps to give a uniform appearance to the shapes. When arranging the stitches for the diamond shape, make sure that a stitch either begins or ends at the extreme tip of the outlined triangle (199). This is most important. If a stitch runs across the point at the corner, the diamond shape will lack precision.

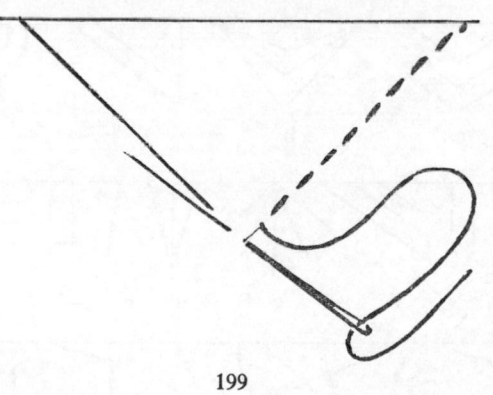

199

With a long length of double thread, well knotted at one end, sew along the pencil outlines from right to left (195). After completing each shape, take the sewing thread over the fold before beginning to sew the adjoining one (200). When several rows are being sewn, cut the thread at the end of each one and knot firmly.

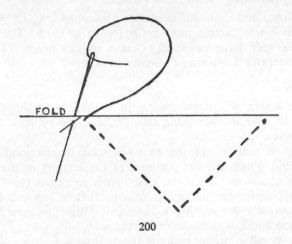

200

When all the sewing is completed pull up the threads as tightly as possible and fasten off.

Dye the entire sample or treat each shape separately.

Other suggestions are :

1. Rows of sewing which radiate from the central point of the outline towards the folded edge may be made, or vice versa.

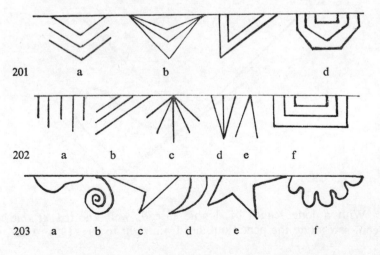

2. One line of sewing, cutting the shape in half, may be made from the fold to the outline, etc. (202d).
3. Several outlines may be sewn, graduating from a very shallow oval or diamond to a very deep one (201b).

2 (*d*) Other Shapes

Many shapes can be sewn on double cloth, individually, in rows or in groups in exactly the same way as ovals or diamonds.

The following suggestions are some, but by no means all of the variations which may be made.

(*i*) Petal-shape, leaf-shape and pear-shape (203a, c. e, f).
(*ii*) Deep rectangles and triangles (201c ; 202d, f).
(*iii*) Pentagon, hexagon, octagon, etc. (201d), concentric circles.
(*iv*) Crescent and star shape (203d, e).
(*v*) Deep points or odd lines of sewing either at right angles to the fold or radiating to or from it, singly or in groups (201a ; 202a, b, c, d, e).
(*vi*) Double spirals (203b) and herringbone effects, etc. (202b).

2 (*e*) A Square

Textured squares

Method

Make a templet of the required square cut in half diagonally (204).

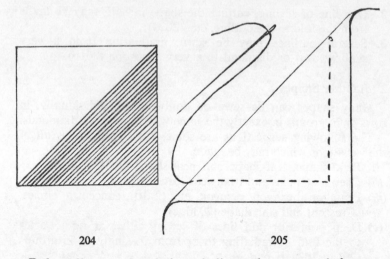

204   205

Rule a line on the cloth to indicate the centre of the proposed square. As the square is halved diagonally, the centre
line must be drawn on the cloth at an angle of 45 deg. to the
selvedge. Fold the cloth over double along this line. Mark round
the templet which is placed at the fold and sew along the outline, making a sharp right-angled corner (205). Knot each end
of the thread and tighten (206). Fasten off. Dye as required.

For a textured square, bind the shape (207, 208) The squares
may be sewn in different ways (209, 210, 211). Rows of squares
may be arranged on the cloth (212).

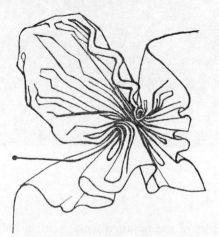

206

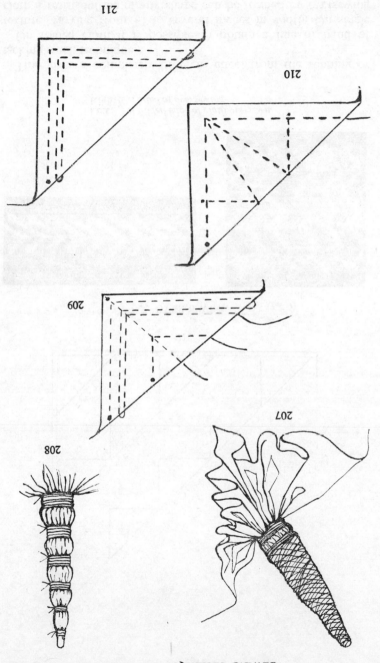

207

208

209

210

211

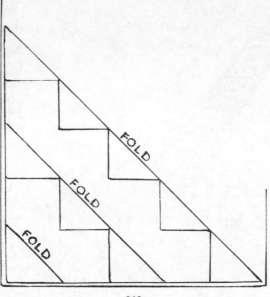

212

3. OVERSEWING

Left: *A folded edge of cloth oversewn*
Right: *A band of oversewing*

This gives a completely different effect from the running or tacking stitch technique.

On folded cloth it is possible to obtain a line or band of texture, varying from $\frac{1}{8}''$ to several inches in width. On single cloth a resist outline of any shape can be formed by oversewing

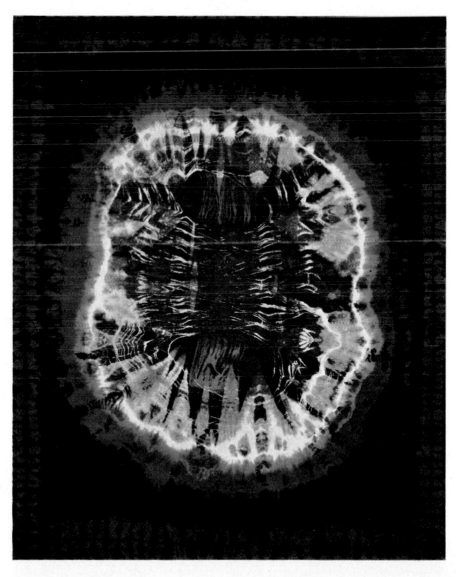

PLATE 5

Blue clump design: section from a repeat pattern obtained by binding large pieces of cork in the fabric

PLATE 6

A variety of diamond-shaped spots on silk, produced by pulling the cloth on the cross while binding

PLATE 7

Cloth 1 yard wide. The herringbone effect (Fig. 202b) is a variation of the running stitch on double cloth method

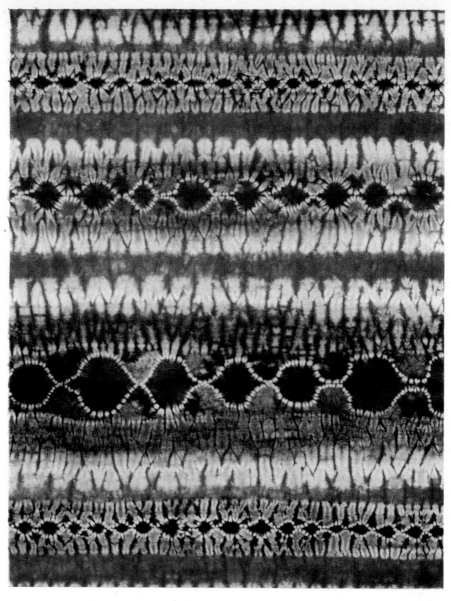

PLATE 8

Section from a repeat pattern formed by tacking stitches on horizontal tucks

PLATE 9

(a) A sample of silk fabric showing the spiral tube method with a horizontal tuck

(b) This rectangle of silk was folded lengthwise, then across. A triangle was tacked against the fold and binding added

PLATE 10

Folding and binding. Direct dyes

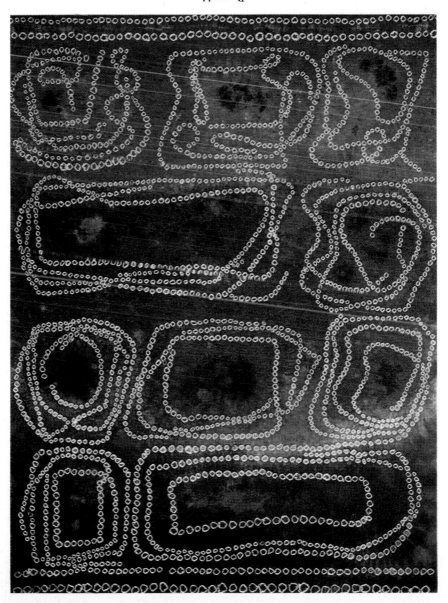

PLATE 11

Wall hanging. Vat dyes. Tiny stones (shingle) tied into cloth. See p. 47

PLATE 12

Cloth: unbleached calico, washed several times. Method: spiral tube, and then reversed for second colour. Vat dyes

along the line, and pulling up the thread before dyeing. This method may be regarded as a tie-and-dye " drawing line."

3 (a) A Line of Oversewing

There are two ways of tackling this particular method.
1. A folded edge of cloth is oversewn.
2. A very narrow flat tuck on the single cloth is oversewn.

Method 1

Draw the required line on the cloth. Crease along it and fold the cloth over double. Use single or double thread according to the length of the line to be sewn. Knot the thread, which should be longer than the distance to be sewn. If this is not possible overlap one or two stitches when making the join, otherwise there will be a gap in the dyed texture (152a and b).

Beginning at the left side of the sample sew over and over the folded edge of cloth (213). If a regular line of texture is aimed at, all the stitches should be equal in size and the same distance apart. Otherwise the size and placing of the stitches may vary according to the needs of the design.

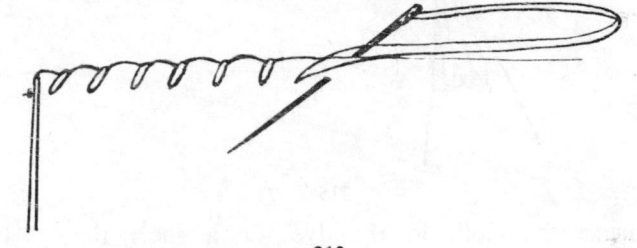

213

After sewing a few inches, begin to draw up the thread slightly, so that instead of wrapping round the cloth, it is straightened out and taut. The cloth will then form into coils round the thread—looking very much like a cord (214).

214

Oversew to the end of the row and if the thread is cut, make a knot. Sometimes it is advantageous to leave the needle and thread attached to the cloth, to be tightened up later. In this case, use a fresh needle and thread for each line of sewing.

Sew all the lines on the sample. When complete, pull up the threads, on each row. To do this, hold the edge of oversewn cloth in the left hand. Pull the sewing thread to the right so that the cloth slides along it and gradually bunches up at the other end. When the thread cannot be tightened any more, fasten off, by backstitching or by tying the ends from two rows together. If double thread is used, the strands can be separated and tied together for the fastening off.

On fine cloth the folded edges of several lines can be collected together and sewn as one (215).

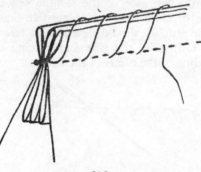

215

Immerse the cloth in the dye for a short time. Rinse thoroughly and do not untie until it is bone dry.

Method 2

Draw the required line on the cloth. Make a crease along the line. Turn the folded edge over as if making a hem, approximately $\frac{1}{8}$—$\frac{1}{4}$ inch deep (216). Now open out the double cloth so that the former hem becomes a tuck, lying flat on the single fabric (217).

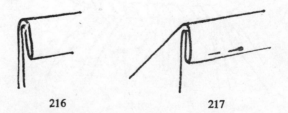

216   217

Pin in place (218). Encircle the tuck, which is now three thicknesses of cloth, with oversewing stitches (219). When all the sewing is completed, draw up the thread so that the cloth is wrapped round it in tightly packed coils. Fasten off, dye, rinse, dry and untie.

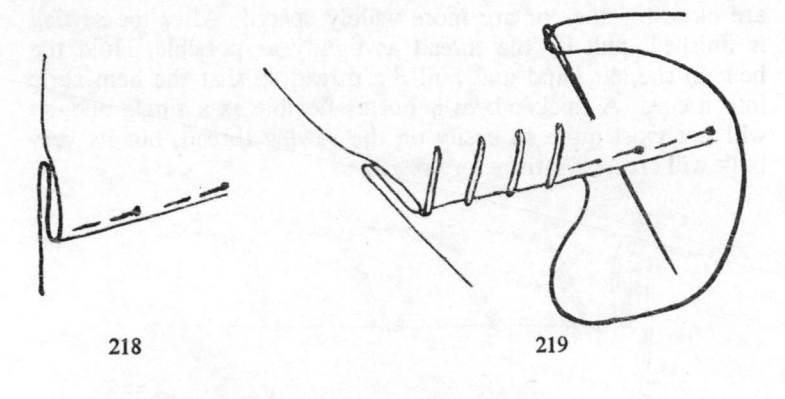

218   219

3 (*b*) A Wider Stripe or Band of Oversewing

A very richly textured resist stripe varying from ½in. to 6 or 8 inches in width can be obtained in this manner, in any direction on the material. Double thread should definitely be used, and, where possible, a piece long enough to complete the row without joining. On a large sample this may not be practicable, in which case overlap one or two stitches, knotting both ends (152a and b).

Method

Rule a line for the centre of the stripe and fold the cloth over double along it. Then turn the edge over as if making a hem (220). This may be from ⅛in. for a fine stripe to ½in. for a larger band of pattern. Pin the hem at intervals.

The hem can be sewn at this stage, but if a wider band of

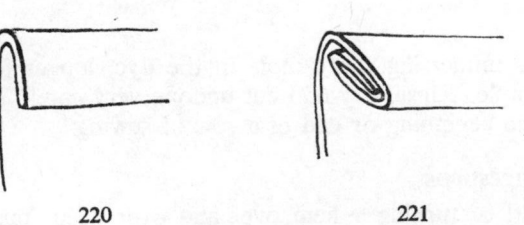

220   221

texture is desired, turn it over again (221) once or twice and pin in place. The hem can be turned over as many as five or six times until the stripe is the width planned.

With a long length of double thread, well knotted, begin to sew over and over the entire hem from left to right (222). The finished texture depends to a large extent on whether the stitches are close together or are more widely spaced. After the sewing is finished, pull up the thread as tightly as possible. Hold the hem in the left hand and pull the thread so that the hem curls into a cord. A thicker hem is not as flexible as a single one, so will not twist quite so easily on the sewing thread, but its very bulk will create a satisfactory resist.

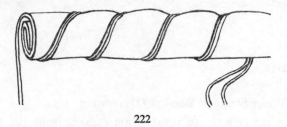

222

When this stage is reached, the addition of an extra row of oversewing, crossing back over the first in the opposite direction, gives a slightly different texture (223). Pull up all the sewing threads and fasten off.

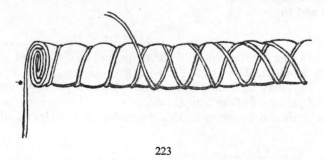

223

Dye by immersing the sample in the dye, longer for a very bulky sample. Rinse, dry and cut undone very carefully, preferably at the beginning or end of a row of sewing.

Other Suggestions

1. Instead of turning a hem over and over itself, make a roll

of the double fabric (224). Pin in place and oversew exactly as if working on the hem.

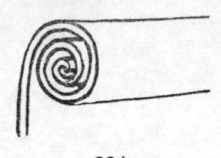

224

2. Add the extra row of sewing before the second dyeing (223).
3. Make alternate narrow and wide bands of texture.
4. Leave the drawing up of alternate stripes until after the first colour has been dyed.
5. The sewing back over the cord-like hem can be arranged to form blocks at intervals along the stripe (225).

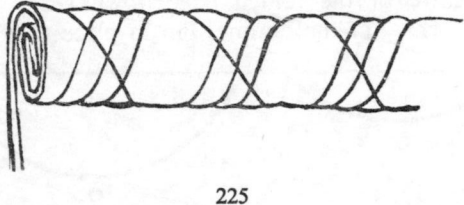

225

6. Two or three hems can be oversewn together, before or after dyeing the first colour.
7. *Matchsticks* can be rolled in the hem.
   Place a matchstick at a fold, roll the double cloth right round it and oversew. Dye, rinse and dry. Before the second colour is dyed more oversewing may be added, or the cloth can be rolled once more round the matchstick and oversewn. The matchstick pattern can be arranged to form blocks, lines, stripes or placed to form circles, squares, etc., or in the shape of flowers and leaves. Each matchstick should be sewn in place separately.
8. Quite a different range of designs, very richly patterned, may be achieved by dyeing narrow oversewn stripes across a sample. Then untie completely and repeat the whole process, making a second layer of wide stripes at right angles to the first. The second colour should be a strong contrast to the previous one. The wider the stripes are made in the second layer, the better the first layer shows through.

3 (c) Oversewn Ovals and Petal Shapes

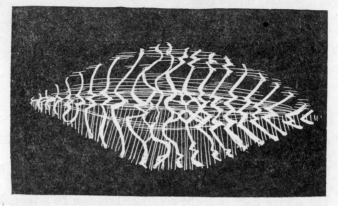

Method

Against a folded edge of cloth draw half the oval shape (226). Roll the centre of the folded edge down (227, 228) until it touches the centre of the outline. Pin in place (229). Unroll the

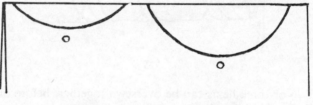

226a   226b

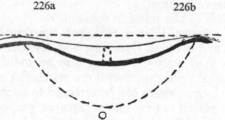

227

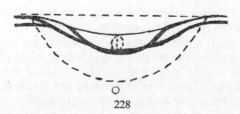

228

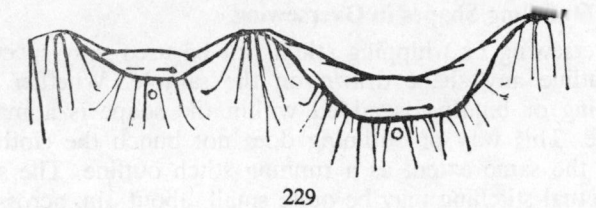

229

cloth on the left side of the pin until the outline is visible. Begin
to oversew it at the fold, but instead of making the stitches all
the same depth, graduate them in size, following the oval outline. Thus the stitches wrap over the rolled edge and draw it
down to the pencil outline. When the centre of the oval is
reached, remove the pin and continue to sew on a decreasing
roll of cloth to the right side of the oval where the outline ends
at the fold (230). Draw up the sewing thread and fasten off
securely.

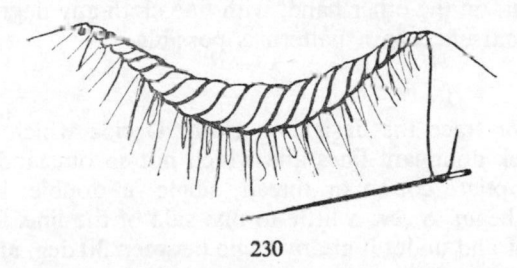

230

This produces an effective oval, petal or leaf shape with quite
amazing texture. These ovals may be large or small, shallow or
deep (226a, 226b). The deeper oval shapes are more difficult to
execute, as the cloth forms into a roll so steeply.

These oversewn ovals may be used singly, in rows on the cloth
or in groups of two, three, four or more radiating from a point
or a line, like the petals of a flower head or leaflets on a stem.
A second line of oversewing may be made, going back over the
first row in the opposite direction (231). Dye as required.

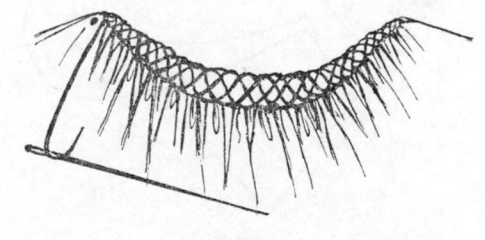

231

3 (d) Outlining Shapes in Oversewing

Oversewing or whipping stitch can be used very successfully to outline any shape drawn on the sample. Whether further stitching or binding is added within the shape is a matter of choice. This way of outlining does not bunch the cloth up to quite the same extent as a running stitch outline. The scale of the actual stitching may be quite small, about ⅛in. across, using single or double Sylko, or up to ½in. wide, with double thread. The width of the stitches, that is the amount of cloth picked up on the needle, each time it is inserted into the cloth, decides the thickness of the outline, and their density determines the tone. For instance, a clear-cut resist outline will need more stitches per inch than a medium toned contour.

Variation in the thickness and tone of the lines should be exploited in working out designs (233).

It is almost impossible to get fine delicate designs on coarse fabric, but, on the other hand, with fine cloth any degree of fineness or coarseness in a pattern is possible.

Method

Draw or trace the design on cloth. Decide which are to be made thick dominant lines and which not so outstanding. With the appropriate cotton or thread, single or double, knotted at one end, begin to sew a little to one side of the line. Take each stitch over and under it at any angle between 30 deg. and 60 deg.

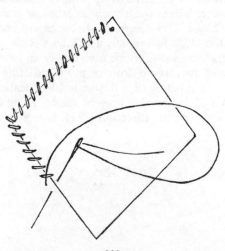

PLATE 13

Panel, approx. 19½ × 20½ in.   Running stitches on double and single cloth

Leopard: outline oversewn; areas of running stitch texture. Spots obtained by tying pearl barley in the clumps

PLATE 14

Two folded squares. That on the right is produced as in Diag. 117

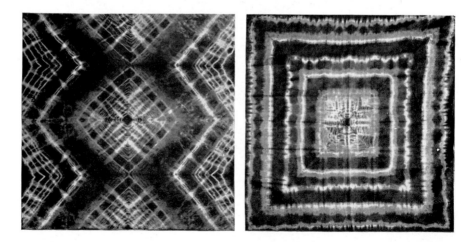

Continue to oversew in this manner (232), keeping the stitches uniform in size and direction, except where adjustments are necessary, following curves or angles in the outline (232, 233). Partially tighten the thread after every one or two inches of sewing. This enables the shape to be drawn up more easily later, besides making the thread go farther. Knot the end of thread whenever it is cut. If a join has to be made, overlap one stitch without tying the threads together (152a and b). Make sure each end has a knot. Quite often it is an advantage to work with several needles and threads on one sample, especially if the lines of sewing overlap or one shape is within another. Then, instead of completing each line, two or three can be sewn concurrently. Keep all the knots on one side of the cloth, that is all on the front or all on the back of the sample (233).

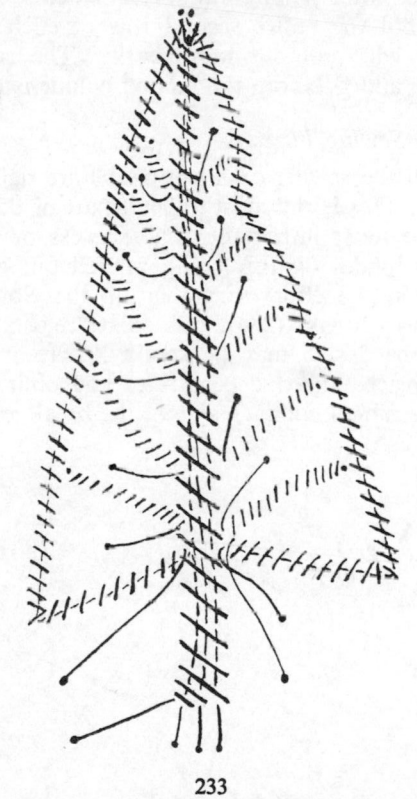

233

A very fine resist outline may be obtained by a double row of tiny stitches carried out in single or double Sylko. In the first row make the stitches to just span the pencil line. Pull up the thread gently after every three or four stitches so that the cloth covers the outline. When the end of the line is reached, double back over it in the opposite direction with a second row of stitches, tightening up the thread at the same time. When the sewing is finished, pull up the thread very gently so that it does not break. Fasten off with a backstitch, or ease up the knot made at the beginning until it is long enough to tie with the second end. This line will not need any further tightening. This is a very useful feature, as it can be used for the parts of the design where the cloth must be kept flat. The only disadvantage is that it is much more difficult to unpick after being dyed.

To do this without making a hole in the fabric, snip the fastening-off knot and loosen the Sylko stitches by inserting the eye of a needle. After pulling out several stitches cut the thread. Repeat this until the entire second row of stiches is released. The first row will pull out more easily. The second row of stitches can be added before the second colour is dyed.

Tightening the Sewing Threads

Complete all the sewing on a sample before tightening up the threads finally. This is the most difficult part of the sewing technique, and the most important. The success or failure of the whole process hinges on this being carried out efficiently.

Sometimes, in the effort to gather up the cloth really compactly the thread breaks (234). Immediate reinstatement should be made, or the design may be spoilt. Where a thread breaks and is not replaced the dye penetrates and obliterates the outline. Where possible knot each side of the break and tie the ends together (235, 236).

234

235

236

When some stitches have slipped, if the threads can be pulled long enough knot one end of the break, then thread the other in a needle to sew in any missing stitches and fasten off (236). If the two ends of the break are very short and there is not enough spare thread to draw on (237) to tie a knot (238), link one inside the other (238a). With a separate piece of cotton, oversew the junction of the two broken ends so that they are firmly linked together and cannot pull apart (238b).

237

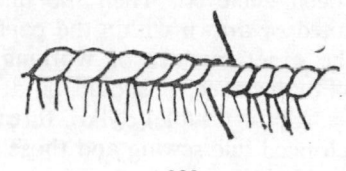

238

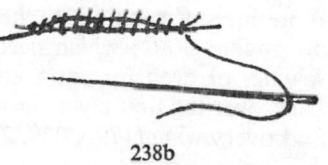

238a   238b

When all the threads have been pulled up tightly and fastened off securely, add binding where it is required. Until a little experience has been gained it is safest to dip the sample in the dye and take it out again immediately. Rinse really thoroughly and make sure the sample is bone dry before untying. The untying needs care and patience (see page 80).

Variations

1. Leave some of the threads to be drawn up before the second or third dyeing.
2. Add binding before dyeing the second colour.
3. Form the sample into a roll and bind before dyeing a second colour. This will give a textured ground.
4. Dye one half a different colour from the other half.
5. Marble or texture the cloth before sewing.
6. Paint a further colour on certain parts with a brush.

4. DESIGNING FOR THE SEWING TECHNIQUE

This, probably more than any other, permits an imaginative interpretation and the development of a personal style. When the essential principles have been mastered, such as pulling up the threads tightly ; fastening off to create a good resist ; knowing the exact effects that different stitches produce, it is then possible to plan designs which make full use of the subtleties of this method.

The scheme in hand, whether for a repeat pattern or for a panel, should be worked out beforehand. On a piece of coloured paper the resist pattern can be drawn with white chalk or poster paint. Alternatively, the resist shapes can be cut out in white paper and moved about on the coloured ground until a pleasing arrangement has been achieved. Then the lines of sewing or texture can be painted or drawn within the paper shapes.

At this stage the exact manner of working out the design should be settled. For instance, it should be decided :
1. Where to use (single or double) Sylko, thread No. 35 or 18.
2. The areas which need fine sewing and those which are better suited to coarser stitches.
3. The kind of outlines. Which parts should have one, two or more lines of running stitches on single cloth (177b, 178b) or on double cloth ; which need single or double rows of oversewing, or even for extra emphasis another layer of stitches back over the first layer; or a combination of running stitches and oversewing (179b, 239, 240, 233).

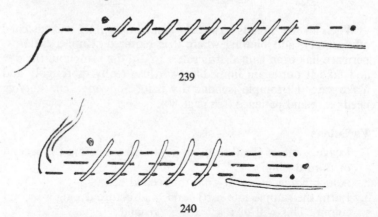

239

240

4. The manner of treating the space inside and outside the sewn shapes should be considered, whether parts should be left plain, textured by binding, sewn texture of running

stitches or oversewing. The direction of the rows of "filling in" must be marked on the design.

5. Determine which threads should be tightened before the first, second or third dyeing.
6. Decide whether certain areas should be dyed a different colour from the rest of the sample.
7. Whether to add binding to give an all-over texture after one or two dyeings. Etc., etc.

Method

Trace or draw the design in pencil on the cloth. Sew the outlines as planned. Complete any other sewing, clump tying, or small bound areas before finally tightening the sewing threads. Dye according to the needs of the design. Rinse, dry and untie.

By this method it is possible to represent birds, fish, animals, people, flowers, trees, plants, buildings, landscapes, etc., if they are worked out in ways suitable for translating into tie-and-dye.

In a complicated design it is very easy to miss a few smaller threads during the tightening-up process. One way of overcoming this is to snip the knot from each end of thread after it has been tied or fastened off. In this way it is possible, by running the fingers over the surface of sewing, to detect any knotted end that still remains. If any knots do remain there is a thread or line of sewing somewhere that still needs to be pulled up. Should this be missed, there will be a gap in the design where that particular thread was ineffectual in forming a resist.

Before finally dyeing, examine both sides of the sample to see if there are any signs of loose stitches. Where there are any showing insert the eye of a needle into one of the loops, or several if it is easier that way, and lever the threads until the row of sewing can be tightened properly. Cut the threads and tie into knots to fasten off.

If the loop is not long enough to cut and tie, oversew it with another thread so that it cannot slacken.

It is possible to make patterns using a modern sewing machine for the stitching if the tension is slackened so that the machining can be pulled up and undone easily afterwards.

A thick cloth is necessary when used singly, preferably dyed with vat dyes. Rows of machining can be made over cloth which has been formed into a series of closely packed knife or box pleats. The Nigerians use this method to advantage.

Wetting-out before dyeing often improves the resist.

VIII

USING CORDS AND ROPES TO PRODUCE PATTERNS AND TEXTURES

HERE is a list of suggestions:

(*a*) Strips of cloth can be plaited along with string or rope. Bind and dye as required.

(*b*) Twist and coil strips of cloth and rope together to form a cord, wrap round a wood base, bind and dye (241).

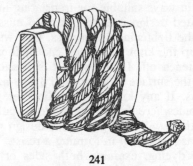

241

(*c*) A strip of cloth can be wrapped round a very thick rope which has been knotted at intervals. Wrap the cloth round the rope diagonally (242) or make it into a tube enclosing the rope (243). Bind the cloth to the rope, in between the knots, and place criss-cross binding over the bulge which includes the knot (244). Dye as required.

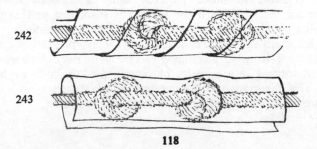

242

243

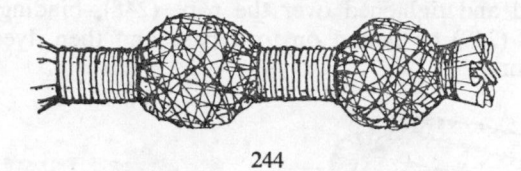

244

(*d*) A strip of cloth and a length of rope can be knotted to-gether at intervals (245). Bind and dye.

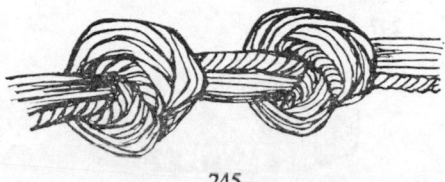

245

(*e*) Any of the above may be prepared and dyed, then bound on to a wooden base, in a flat coil ; in tight flat loops ; or twisted over and over the base itself (246). Add binding before dyeing the second colour.

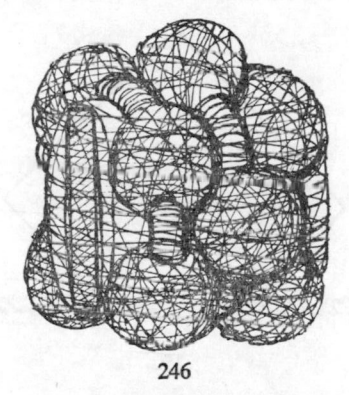

246

(*f*) A sample which has been previously sewn with rows of running stitches (on single or double cloth) can be drawn up to form a tube and a thick rope placed inside. The rope can be knotted before being used. Bind the tube and dye once or twice. Rinse, dry and untie.

(*g*) Thick rope can be sewn in between two layers of cloth in the manner of quilting or it may be threaded through a large tuck made in the cloth, as described for ruching (247). The cloth is gathered and tightened over the rope (248), binding or sew-ing added (249) or bound on to a base and then dyed one or more colours.

247   248

249

(*h*) A piece of rope can be rolled inside a square of cloth diagonally, beginning at one corner (250). Or the cloth can be folded in half diagonally (251), then the rope placed along the fold and the two rolled into a tube (252) until the corner of the

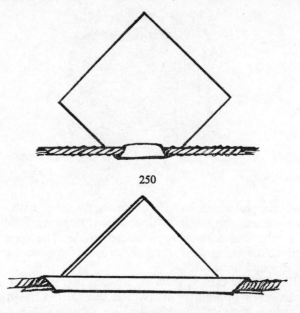

250

251

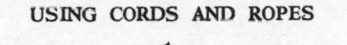

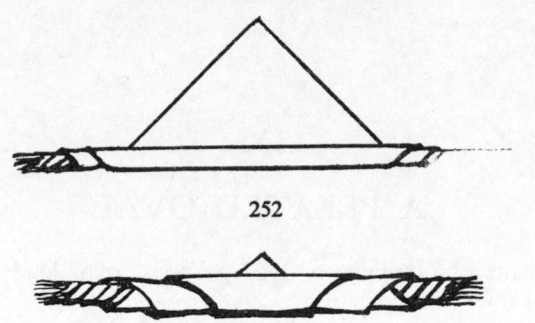

252

253

triangle is reached (253). Fold into one or more loops and bind (254, 255).

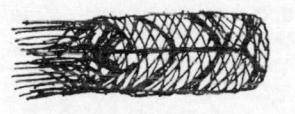

254   255

In most cases these methods can be carried out with very small strips of cloth which can later be joined together, or used as scarves. Much larger pieces of cloth can be used for the above methods, but extra binding or manipulation of the cloth or ropes might be necessary, otherwise there would not be enough pattern interest created.

IX

A PLEATED OVAL

THIS means of obtaining a dyed or resist oval lends itself to numerous interpretations.
1. Each oval can be pleated, bound and dyed as a separate shape on a dyed or undyed ground.
2. An oval shape can be reserved on a dyed ground.
3. Several individual shapes can be grouped together in any direction to form floral and leaf designs.
4. The oval can be extended to form diamond and circular shapes, or elongated to produce narrow stripes, suitable for depicting stems and narrow leaves.

Method

Where any repetition of the oval occurs a templet should be made, by halving the shape lengthwise.

Fold the cloth over double along the centre of the required oval. Place the straight edge of the templet to the folded edge of the fabric. Mark round the templet. Keep the double cloth in position with pins or a few tacking stitches (256).

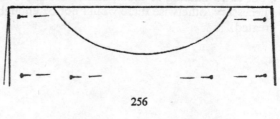

256

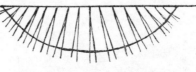

257

Each oval is now ready to be folded into small pleats, arranged in the manner of a fan (257). Beginning at the folded edge, and

122

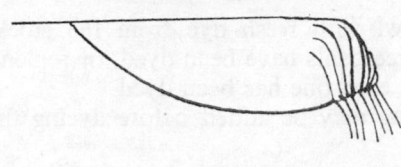

258

working along the pencil line from right to left (258), make a
series of pleats, approximately $\frac{1}{8}$in. to $\frac{1}{2}$in. across, with the
thumbs and forefingers (259). This means that the curved pencil
outline is now pleated up closely and is straightened out, whereas the straight folded edge of cloth is radiating from it in a
semi-circle like a fan. Make a firm but narrow binding on the
pencil line, and fasten off (260). From this point the pattern is
determined by the manner of dyeing and the amount of binding
applied to the ovals.

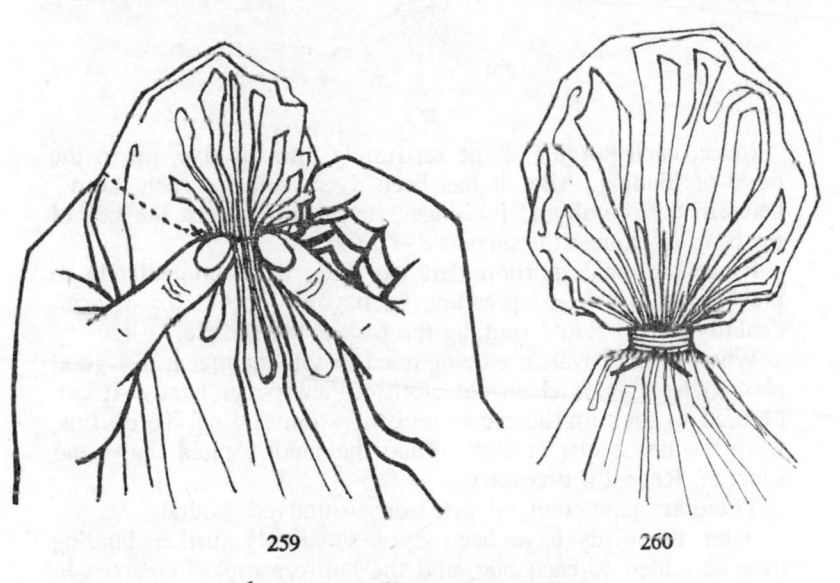

259   260

1. TO DYE INDIVIDUAL OVALS

When these pleated ovals are being treated separately they
need careful and exact dyeing. For this process a small shallow
bowl is recommended. Mix up the full quantity of dye liquor
needed for the whole sample in a separate vessel. Make the
depth of the dye in the small bowl equivalent to the height of
the "fan-like" pleats, from the binding to the highest point
(108a and b).

Refill the bowl with fresh dye from the stock vessel after every two or three ovals have been dyed, or replenish by adding a little dye after each one has been dyed.

A little binding may be added before dyeing the first colour if desired (261).

261

Invert each fan-like shape separately into the dye, up to the ridge of binding. After it has been dyed, squeeze each "fan" between the thumb and forefinger, or press it against the side of the bowl to express the surplus dye (109).

Rinse the small portion that has been dyed immediately to prevent the dye from spreading up beyond the binding or accidentally touching and staining the rest of the sample.

When several ovals are being dyed in this manner it is a good plan to have some clean old cloth or newspaper handy. It can be used to soak up the excess moisture after rinsing. To do this, wrap the newspaper or cloth round the small pleated shape and squeeze. Repeat if necessary.

There are now coloured ovals on an undyed ground.

After the ovals have been dyed separately further binding may be added to each one, and the entire sample immersed in a second dye. This gives a dyed oval on a ground of a different colour. Rinse and dry.

A third colour can be introduced by dipping the extreme tips of the small fan shapes in a darker or brighter dye. This gives the impression of a central vein to each oval. This darker dye on the tips can be applied with a brush.

The extreme edges of the dyed ovals may be brushed over with bleach.

Rinse thoroughly, dry and untie.

2. RESIST OVALS ON A DYED GROUND

Method

Mark out, pleat and bind the ovals as described for No. 1.

The amount of binding each individual fan-like shape receives will decide the kind of resist effect produced.

(*a*) A clear-cut solid resist oval is formed if the binding covers the shape completely in a double layer; or the bound shape is painted over with melted wax and a cold dye used.

(*b*) A partial resist will be formed with lattice or open binding giving a texture somewhat resembling the veins of a leaf (262).

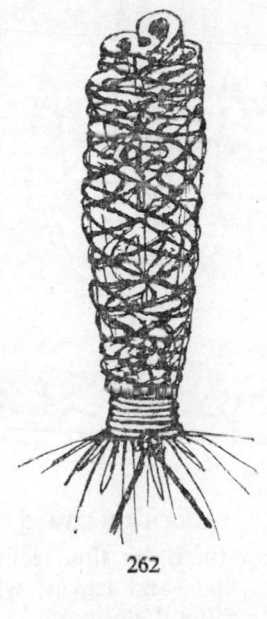

262

(*c*) A resist outline of the oval like a letter O is all that remains if the binding is confined to a narrow band along the pencil line (260).

Although several colours may be used this method gives pleasing results if the sample is dyed once, relying for its effect on the variety of textures formed by the different kinds of binding. A full rich colour is preferable in this case to give plenty of contrast between the dyed and the resist areas.

After binding immerse the whole sample in the dyebath. Rinse and dry. Add more binding before dyeing a second or third colour. Rinse, dry and untie. Iron off any wax.

Rinse after untying if necessary.

Any of the ovals can be repeated at intervals over the cloth to form an all-over pattern (263).

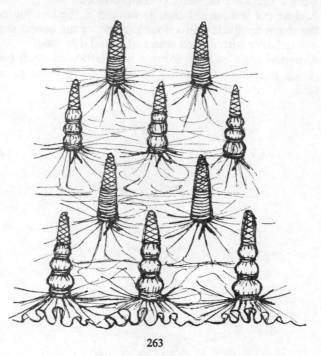

263

3. GROUPS OF OVALS

The oval shapes produced by this technique can easily be adapted to represent petals and leaves, which, when suitably grouped, give attractive floral designs. As each petal or leaf must be big enough to pleat and bind separately, it is rather difficult to work on too small a scale.

Method

Draw the entire design on the fabric. Fold each leaf and petal or oval in half lengthwise, then pleat and bind as described for No. 1.

When making several separate petals for a flower it may be

necessary to make a small binding in the centre to connect them together.

Dye according to the requirements of the design.

4. Variations on the Basic Shape

Other shapes produced by this method are carried out in exactly the same way as the oval, the only difference being the shape marked on the cloth below the central fold in the first place, along which the pleats are made. Vary the size of the shapes as required.

4 (a) Diamond

Method

Draw in pencil below the central fold of cloth a shallow triangle, equivalent to the diamond cut in half lengthwise, or across the shorter diagonal. This means that the wider angle of the diamond (unless they are all equal) becomes the angle at the apex of the triangle (264).

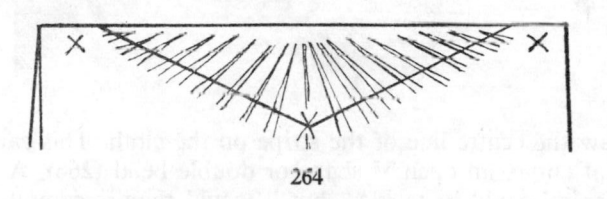

264

Put a pin or tacking stitch X in the double cloth and at the apex of the triangle to prevent the underside from slipping while the pleating process is carried out. Pleat the cloth as in No. 1, giving special care to the apex of the triangle which has to be flattened out and brought into line with the rest of the outline. Bind along the pencil line and add more for a textured shape as for a pleated oval.

Dye as required.

4 (b) A Narrow Pleated Strip

Method

Along a folded edge of cloth which represents the central line of the stripe mark half the outline of the shape (265b).

Crease the double cloth into small pleats from right to left

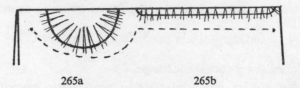

265a   265b

along the pencil line, to form a compact mass. Place a narrow but firm binding round the pleated bundle, to coincide with the pencil line. Add binding if a wider resist area is required.

Dye, rinse, dry and untie.

This method is useful for depicting narrow leaves or stems. It can also be introduced as a motif in a repeat design.

4 (c) A Stripe that Changes Direction

Draw the centre line of the stripe on the cloth. This can be a gradual curve, an open V shape or double bend (266). A large-scale spiral could be tackled, but it would require careful handling and would need to be pinned at intervals. A large hollow circle or oval, in the shape of an " O," is possible in this method.

Make a crease along the pencil line, which can now be looked on as the central fold. Proceed to bunch up the double cloth into small pleats as in 4(b), just below the folded edge. Secure with a narrow binding just below the fold.

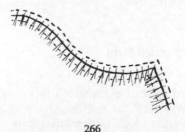

266

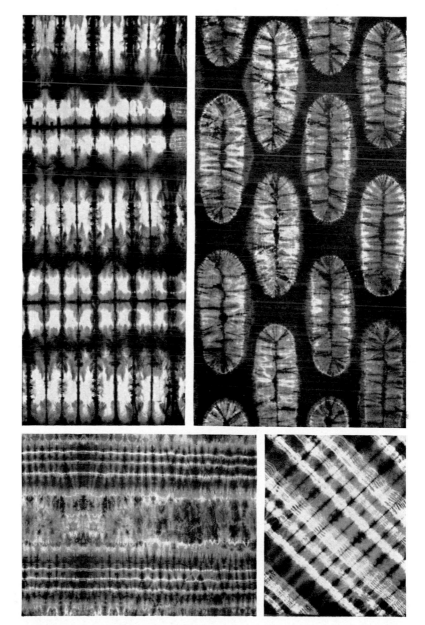

PLATE 15

Top left: *Diagonal stripe, rope technique*
right: *A knotted length of cloth with groups of 3-line bindings*

Bottom left: *Pleated ovals*
right: *Large-scale rope tying*

PLATE 16

Top left: *Pattern composed of bands of ruching with sewn ovals and rows of sewn resist lines*
Right: *Simple stripe*
Bottom left: *Edge stripes with dyed background*
Centre: *Pleated diamond (variation of pleated oval); beneath it, a wide band of oversewing, showing on left effect of extra stitches in the opposite direction*
Right: *Chevron. Spiral tube method 2, see Diags. 306, 307*

Dye the whole sample, or paint dye on the folded edge only. This can be done after the first colour has been dyed. On a sample that has been previously dyed these edges could be bleached.

4 (d) Circle
A circle is made in exactly the same way as an oval, except that a semi-circle is drawn at the folded edge of cloth (265a).

5 Using a Safety-pin for Pleated Ovals
Very much the same effect as pleated ovals, diamonds and circles can be achieved if a large safety-pin is woven in and out at intervals along the pencilled outline from right to left. This forms pleats as shown in Figs. 257, 258 and 264. When the safety-pin has enclosed the complete shape, close it, make a narrow binding immediately below the closed pin to retain the pleats in position, then remove the pin. The sample should now appear as Fig. 260. Bind as required. Repeat for each individual shape.

X

RUCHING

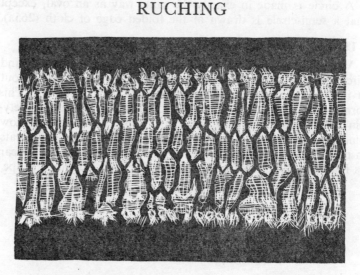

Tuck method, using wooden base with ½ inch square cross-section

RUCHING, as the name suggests, is a means of obtaining patterns by gathering fabric compactly round pieces of wood or any other suitable objects. Binding is added to give stability to the gathers and to help form a richly textured resist stripe.

The kind of base used plays an important part in influencing this texture and determines the width of the stripe. The cross-section of the base, whether circular (267), triangular or rectangular (268), affects the pattern. Pieces of wood are ideal for this purpose as the cloth slides along the smooth surface easily.

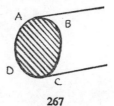

267

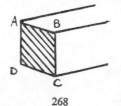

268

Wood, also, is cheap, obtainable in all shapes and sizes and can be used over and over again.

Tuck Method

Select a piece of wood ½in. by ½in. or 1in. by 1in. in section and about 6in. long. A length of broom handle, pencil or ruler, etc., can be used.

A tuck EF must now be made in the cloth, to act as a string-case to enclose the base. It must be slightly bigger than the perimeter of the cross-section of the base ABCD (268). To ascertain its measurement, wrap the cloth or a piece of string round the selected base. Halve the amount taken to enclose the base and add ½in. This gives the width of the tuck or string-case. Rule a line on the cloth to represent the centre of the stripe, crease and fold over double. Rule another line the same distance from the folded edge as the width of the tuck EF. Sew a row of tacking stitches on double cloth along this line, knotting the thread at the beginning and end (269). Push the wood into the tuck so formed (270), and pull up the tacking stitches (271). Pack the ruched fabric solidly at one end of the base.

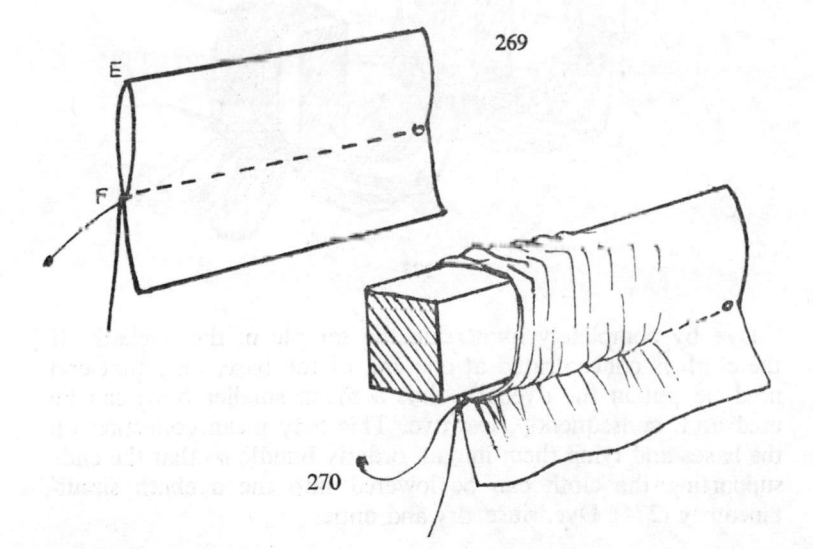

269

270

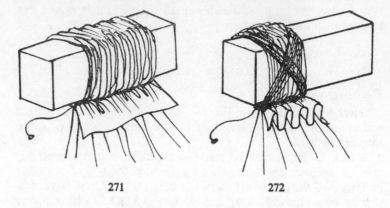

271   272

The whole success of the technique hinges on this part of the operation. The more tightly packed the ruching is the more successful and definite the pattern will be. Bind round the ruching (272) so that it will resist the dye more effectively. The drawn-up sewing threads can be used for this purpose.

Repeat this procedure over the sample, using a separate base and string-case for each stripe (273).

273

Dye by completely immersing the sample in the dyebath. It the cloth is concentrated at one end of the base, only that end need be put in the dyebath, thus a much smaller bowl can be used and, consequently, less dye. This may mean collecting up the bases and tying them into an orderly bundle so that the ends supporting the cloth can be lowered into the dyebath simultaneously (274). Dye, rinse, dry and untie.

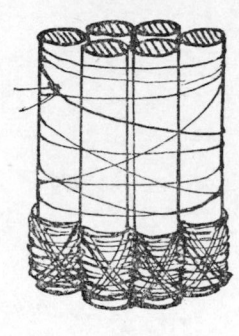

274

Variations

1. Add more binding and dye a second colour.
2. Sew all the tucks for the string-cases, but leave alternate ones empty. Dye, rinse and dry. Insert the remaining bases before dyeing a second colour.
3. Insert the bases and tighten thread. Add binding after the first colour has been dyed, then dye a second colour.
4. Apply the second dye with a brush on the ruched areas only.
5. Make an alternate wide and narrow stripe by using a thick and thin base.
6. Bind the bases containing the ruchings together in pairs before dyeing a second colour.
7. Outline the top edge of the tuck with a row of tacking stitches, making another minute tuck which can be over-sewn (275) and put extra rows of stitches at the lower end (276). The string-case may have several small sewn tucks on each side (277). The sewing threads should not be drawn up until after the base has been inserted in the main tuck.

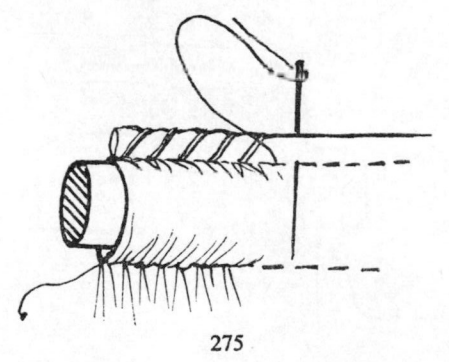

275

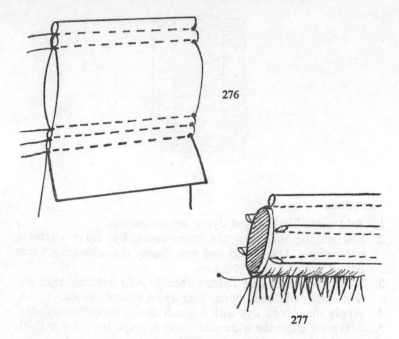

276

277

8. Make a double-decker ruching, using a very narrow and a
   wider base in the same tuck (278). Sew a tuck below the
   folded edge big enough to enclose the narrow base, using one
   or several rows of sewing. Make a second row or band of
   tacking stitches, far enough away from the first, so that the
   second tuck will accommodate the wider base. Insert both
   bases, pull up the threads, bind and dye. The top ruching
   can be dyed a different colour from the lower one.

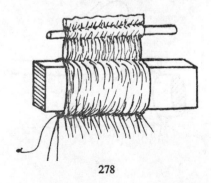

278

Making a String-case on Double Cloth

It is possible to make a string-case by sewing together two separate pieces of cloth or folding one length in half (279). A square of cloth can be folded over diagonally to form a double triangle (279a).

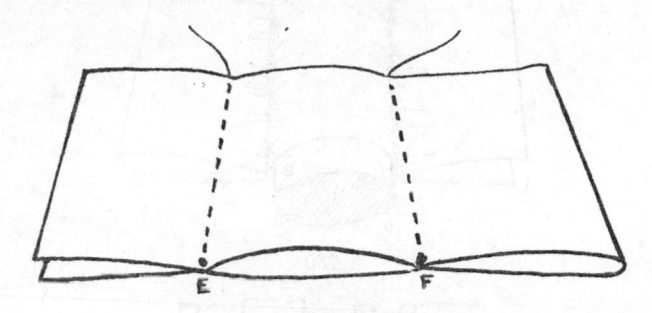

279

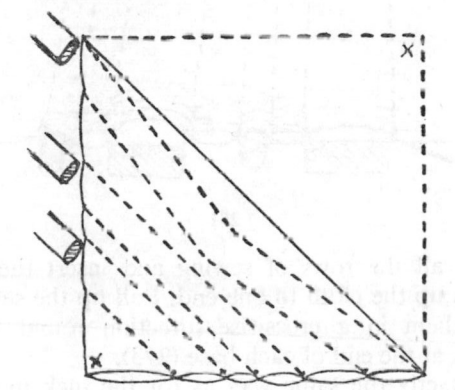

279a

Method

Pin the two halves of cloth together accurately. Mark on one side of the double cloth where the rows of sewing are to be placed. The tunnel EF made between two rows of sewing provides the string-case and must be made wide enough, therefore, to enclose the base (279). To estimate this distance halve the measurement of the perimeter of the cross-section of the base ABCD and add ½in.

By this method the rows of ruching can be placed closer

together than by the tuck method. It is probably more useful
for a regular repeat pattern (281).

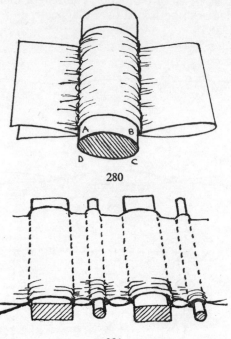

280

281

Complete all the rows of sewing and insert the bases (280,
281). Bunch up the cloth to one end. Pull up the sewing threads
and wrap them in a crosswise direction round the mass of
ruched cloth at the end of each base (273).

Dye in exactly the same way as for the tuck method.

OVAL AND DIAMOND PATTERNS

Some quite magnificent designs can be created by adapting
the ruching technique to form large scale oval and diamond
patterns. In this case much wider and longer pieces of wood
are required. The string-cases may be sewn across, lengthwise
or diagonally on the cloth.

Both the tuck and double cloth methods may be used.

Method

Determine the width of the string-cases EF (see above). If

the pattern is very large, allow half the perimeter of the cross-section ABCD, plus ¾in. to 1in.

Tuck Method

Mark the position of the string-cases on the sample.

Fold the cloth over double. Draw half of the inner oval or diamond shape E, so that the central line coincides with the folded edge of the cloth (282 and 283). Still further below this, draw the outer edge of the half oval or diamond outline F.

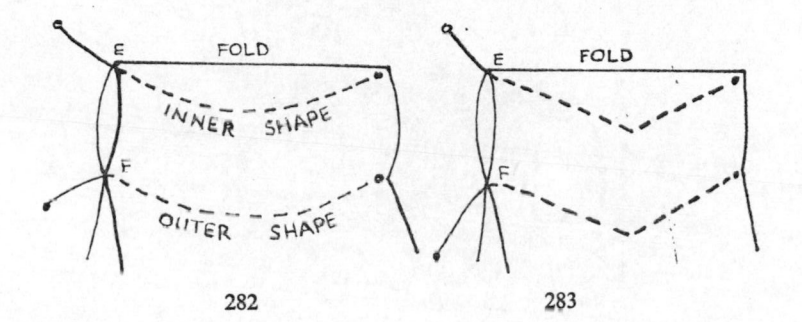

282   283

This second line follows the direction of the first, but at a distance away from it equal to the width of the string-case EF. If there are several ovals or diamonds, cut templates (284, 285).

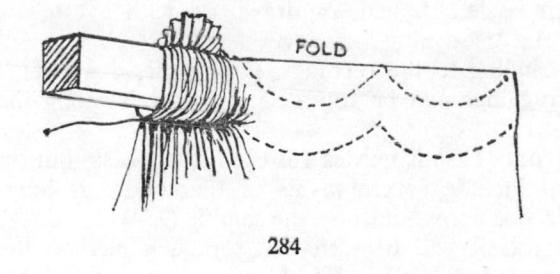

284

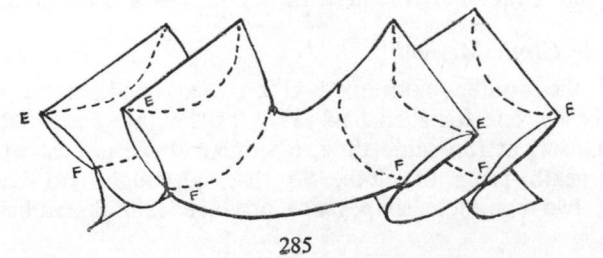

285

On the double cloth sew along both sets of pencil lines with double thread, making a firm knot at each end (282, 283).

Very carefully push the base into the curved or V-shaped string-case now formed (284), and draw up the sewing threads (286). Gradually ease the cloth to one end of the base until there is a firm mass of bunched-up ruching.

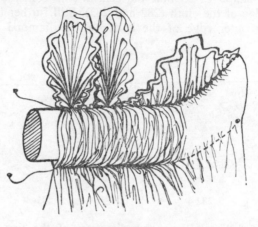

286

The centre of the oval or diamond will now be projecting up above the ruching on the base, in a fan-like shape (286). This can be left, bound, or drawn up with oversewing before or after the first dyeing.

Add binding to the ruchings. Dye, rinse, dry and untie.

The ruchings can be repeated at intervals along the sample (285).

A separate base is needed for each string-case, but one string-case can include several ovals or diamonds, as long as they are all in line across or down the sample (284).

From this it will be seen that the tuck method produces a complete oval or diamond with one string-case and base (285).

Double Cloth Method

By the double cloth method an oval or diamond requires two bases, one for each half (287), as they are sewn flat on the cloth. But, at the same time, a similar shape is created on the underneath piece of cloth. So that, although two bases are used, two complete shapes are produced simultaneously (287, 288).

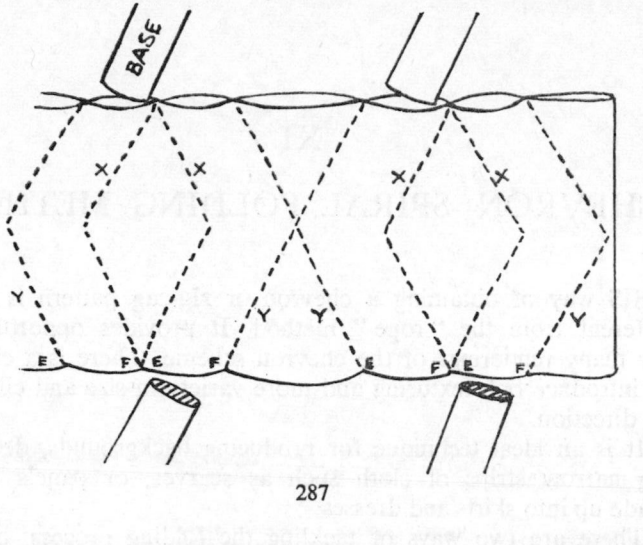

287

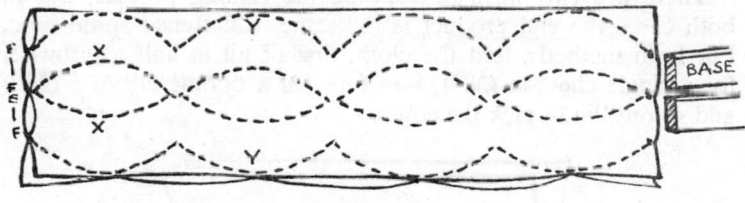

288

Pin the two halves of the cloth together.

Find the width of the string-case EF.

Mark the whole of the inner oval or diamond X on the cloth where required. Parallel to this and at a distance away from it equal to EF, draw the outer shape Y. Tack along the pencil lines (287, 288), insert bases, draw up sewing threads, and add binding. Dye as required.

XI

CHEVRON–SPIRAL FOLDING METHOD

THIS way of obtaining a chevron or zig-zag pattern is quite different from the "rope" method. It provides opportunities for many renderings of the chevron scheme. There is a chance to introduce rich texturing and more variety in size and changes of direction.

It is an ideal technique for producing backgrounds, decorating narrow strips of cloth such as scarves, or panels to be made up into skirts and dresses.

There are two ways of tackling the folding process, but in both cases the end product is the same, a flattened spiral tube. For both methods, fold the cloth, first of all in half lengthwise, for a single chevron (289), into four for a double chevron (290) and so on. Pin or tack the edges.

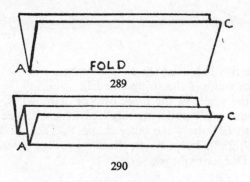

289

290

Method 1

A ruler or pencil (for small samples) (291 and 292), a strip of plywood, thick cardboard, or a length of broom handle (for larger pieces of cloth) (293 and 294), is required as a base round which to wind the sample. Hold corner A firmly in place at one end of the base (293, 295), while the rest of the sample is wound round it (294, 296) to form a spiral tube (297). Pin or tack corner C in place (297). Put pins at intervals along the tube.

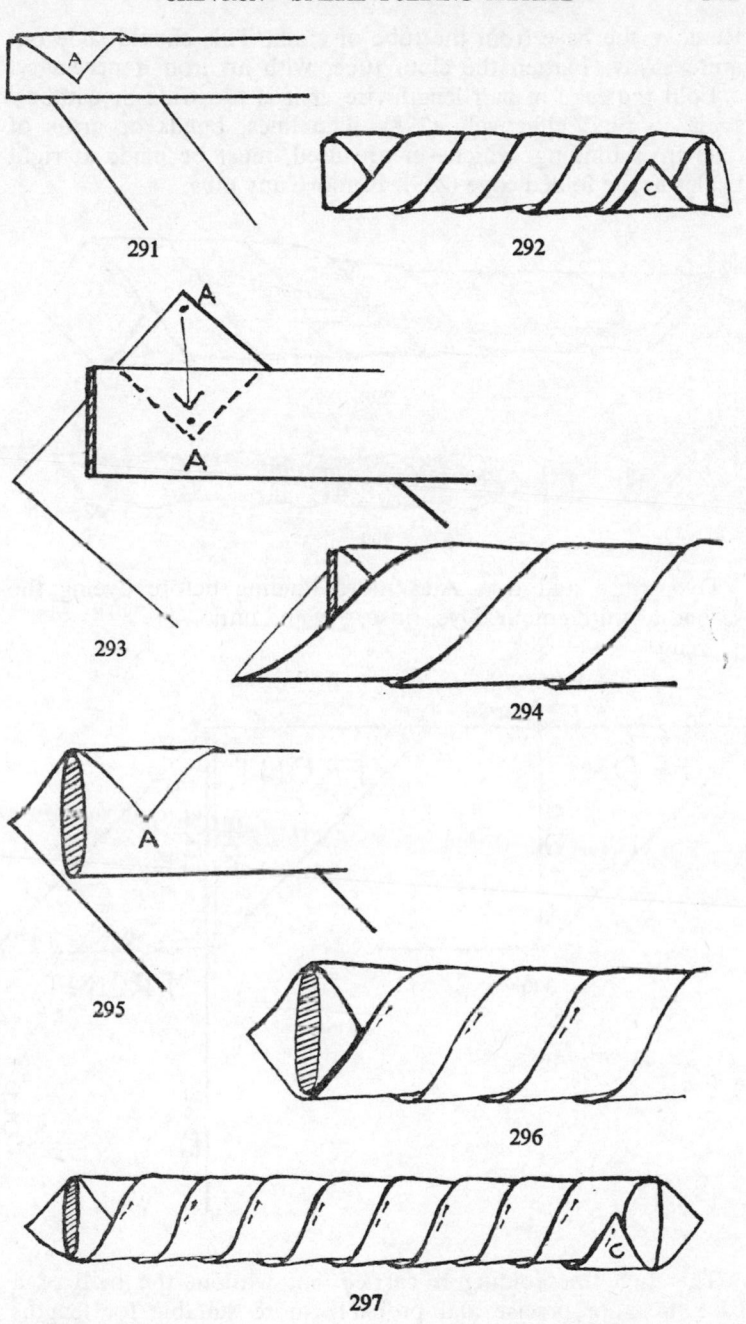

291

292

293

294

295

296

297

Remove the base from the tube of cloth. This should slide out quite easily. Flatten the cloth tube, with an iron if necessary.

Fold the tube in half lengthwise, if it is too wide or cumbersome to bind effectively (298). The lines, bands or areas of criss-cross binding, whichever are used, must be made at right angles to the folded edge (299). Remove any pins.

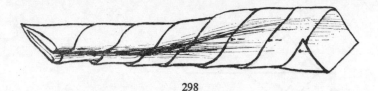

298

299

Dye, rinse and dry. Add more binding before dyeing the second or third colour. Dye, rinse, dry and untie.

Method 2

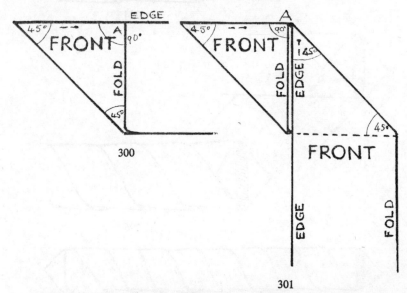

300

301

This time the folding is carried out without the help of a base, is more precise and probably more suitable for lengths of cloth than method No. 1. It is possible to begin at either end. Fold corner A over and pin to the selvedge edge so that a right-angled triangle is formed (300). Fold down the cloth at corner A at an angle of 45 deg. so that the selvedge is parallel to, and just touches the folded edge. Crease and pin in place (301). Turn the whole sample over so that the present top surface is face downwards.

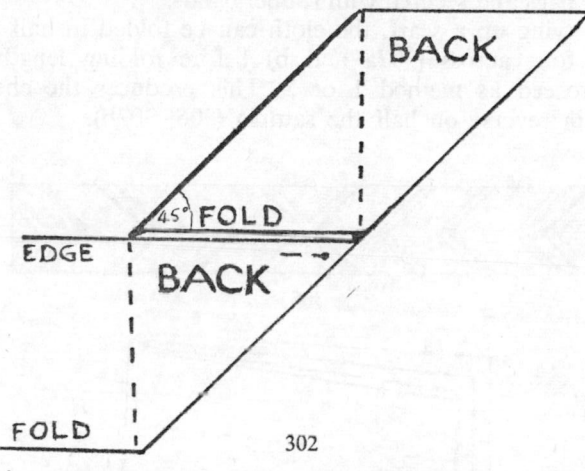

302

Again, turn the next piece of selvedge over at 45 deg. so that it touches the folded edge of the previous layer (302). Pin in place and turn the sample back again, so that the original surface is at the top. Continue to turn the selvedge down at 45 deg. until the entire length of cloth is formed into a flattened spiral tube (303).

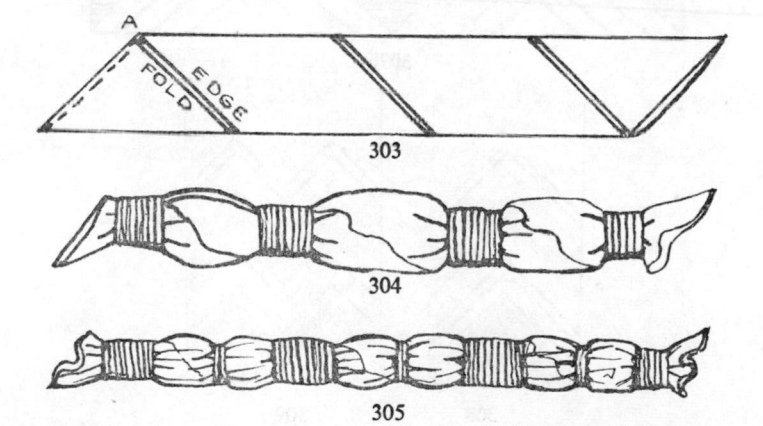

303

304

305

Bind (304) and dye as required. Add more binding for second colour (305). When working on a very long sample, tack the folded tube carefully and bind for about 8–12 ins. at both ends. Roll each end into a ball and tie. Bind a further 6in., roll this on the ball and tie. Work towards the centre from both ends in this way until all the bindings are completed. The balls of tied-up cloth may be enclosed in pieces of old nylon stocking or paper bags and secured with rubber bands.

When tying up a scarf, the cloth can be folded in half (306) or into four across (307a and b) before folding lengthwise. Then proceed as method 1 or 2. This produces the chevron pattern in reverse on half the sample (306, 307b).

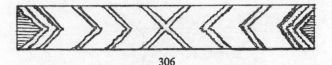

306

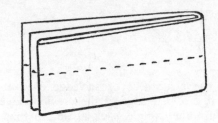

307a

307b

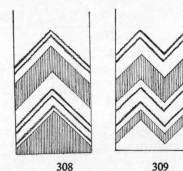

308   309

To dye a border pattern fold the cloth into two (308), three or four (309) thicknesses lengthways and wrap one end *only*, diagonally round the base. Bind for one large chevron or several finer ones by making a wide or several narrow bands of binding respectively (310). The rest of the sample may be left unbound, for a plain ground, or covered with open or crisscross binding for a textured ground. Dye as required.

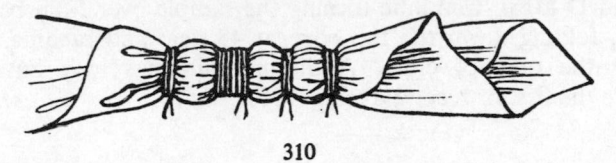

310

The spiral tube method can be used for patterning long but narrow lengths of very fine cloth.

Method

Fold cloth into four or more thicknesses lengthways until it is reduced to approximately 1—2 inches in width. A B is the width of the cloth and A B C D is a square (311).

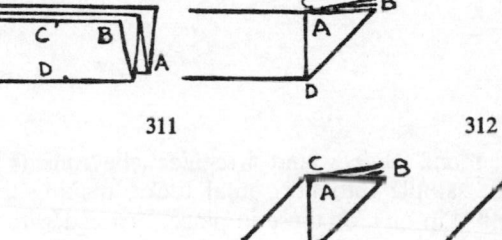

311   312

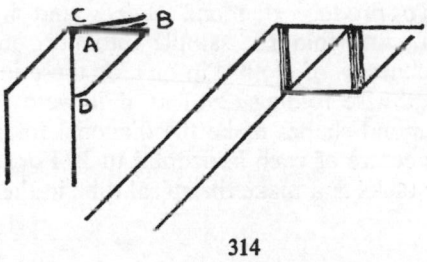

313   314

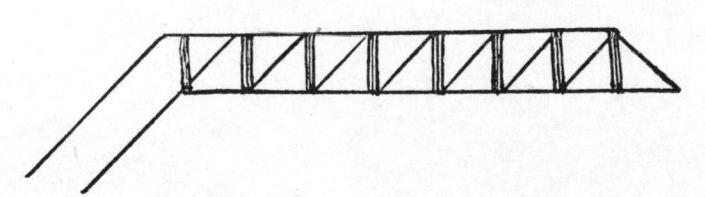

315

At B fold the cloth up at an angle of 45 deg. so that A B is horizontal and in line with the top edge B C (312).

At C fold the cloth downwards at an angle of 45 deg. so that B C becomes vertical and touches A D (313).

Make narrow bindings at A and D at right angles to the new folded edge (314). Now turn the sample over back to front, fold the top edge down at an angle of 45 deg. and bind as at A and D (315). Continue turning the sample over from back to front, folding down the top edge at 45 deg. and binding, right along the tube of cloth. Additional bindings may be made before the first or second dyeing (316).

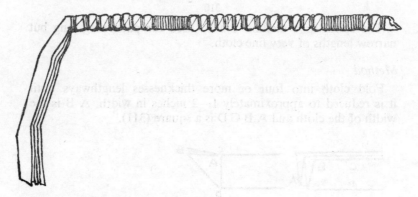

316

To produce diamond shapes and irregular chevrons (Plate 13a), first fold the sample into horizontal tucks, making three thicknesses of cloth. Pin or tack these in place. Proceed with the lengthwise folding (290) as if it were single cloth. To produce diamond shapes make the diagonal folds (300–302) come across the centre of each horizontal tuck. For irregular chevrons ignore the tucks and make the spiral tube in the usual way.

XII

DYED BACKGROUNDS

QUITE simple tie-and-dye patterns are greatly enhanced when carried out on a length of cloth, previously dyed with areas of plain colour or texture. These can be placed at random, or planned to fit in with the proposed design. In the main, background shapes and textures are obtained by adapting the normal methods of tie-dyeing so that larger areas can be patterned more easily and quickly. For the superimposed pattern, really large scale shapes look well, as they form a frame for the background texture.

TEXTURED BACKGROUNDS

(a) Marbling Larger Pieces of Cloth

It is quite possible to dye a length of cloth several yards long with the marbling technique.

Methods

1. *Circles*. Mark out large circles, arranged in a regular repeat, or of varying sizes, placed at chosen spots on the cloth (317). The outlines may be tacked, but this is not essential.

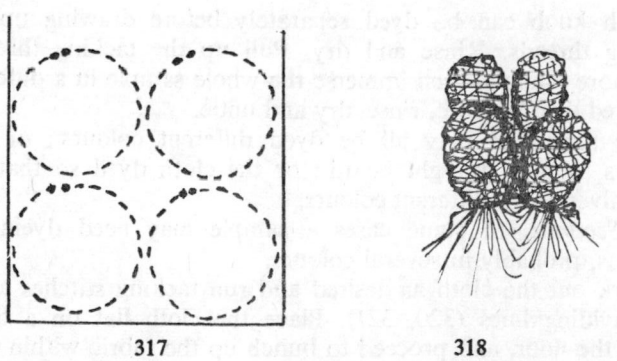

317   318

Bunch up the fabric within each circle into a tight mass and bind it to form a solid knob (318). If the cloth is placed flat on the table, the bunching up process can be carried out more evenly. Each individual knob can be dyed, giving circular patches of marbling on a white ground.

To get an all-over texture, the tacking threads must be drawn up and the cloth in between the knobs bunched up and bound before the whole sample is dyed. Another method of texturing in between the circles, is to bring the two selvedges together to make a tube lengthways, and to add open binding in between the knobs which now project on the outside.

Dye, rinse, dry and untie.

2. *Rectangles.* Make lines of tacking stitches (these can be really large) down the centre and each side of the sample. Run another set of lines across, so that the cloth is divided into large rectangles (319). Bunch up the cloth within each rectangle, for marbling, and bind into a knob (318). Pull up the tacking threads. Dye, rinse and dry.

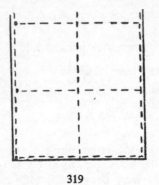

319

Each knob can be dyed separately before drawing up the tacking threads. Rinse and dry. Pull up the tacking threads, add more binding, then immerse the whole sample in a different coloured dye. Squeeze, rinse, dry and untie.

The rectangles may all be dyed different colours; or two colours as in a draught board; or the cloth dyed so that the two halves are of different colours.

3. *Sections.* In some cases a sample may need dyeing in sections, probably in several colours.

Mark out the cloth as desired and run tacking stitches along the dividing lines (320, 321). Place the cloth flat on a table, or on the floor, and proceed to bunch up the fabric within each division, into a solid mass. Bind each mass separately until it is formed into a solid knob. Pull up the tacking stitches and fasten off.

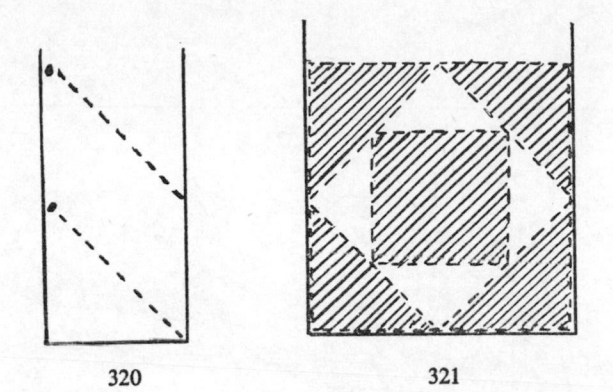

320   321

Dip each knob separately into its particular colour. Rinse and dry. Add more binding if the whole sample is to be immersed in another coloured dye.

4. *Tube*. When all-over marbling texture is preferred, the following method will give very satisfactory results. This is an easy and effective way and one which allows a great deal of latitude, producing sparse or dense pattern, according to the amount of binding added or the length of time left in the dyebath.

Method

Place the cloth flat on a table, or on the floor, and have at hand a reel of cotton.

Beginning at right, pick up points across the cloth at intervals (322) and collect them together in the left hand. Wrap the cotton round this bundle to hold it in place, while the next group of "points" is collected (323). Wrap the cotton round this next bunch, pulling it just tight enough to keep the cloth in a loose roll. Continue in this way, working along the cloth, forming it into a "sausage." Keep the right side on the outside all along the tube (324).

After the first process the "sausage" of material will be approximately one-third of its original length. Using stronger thread or fine string, rebind the loosely bunched tube firmly, from one end to the other, and then back again to the beginning with open criss-cross binding. Repeat this backward and

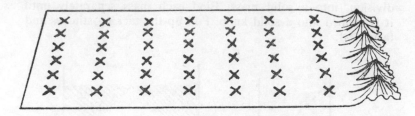

322

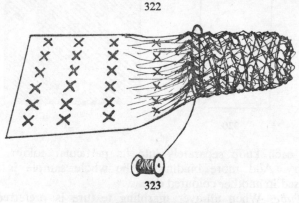

323

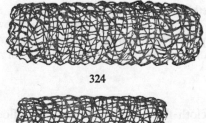

324

325

forward binding until a very tight "sausage," still further reduced in size, is produced (325).

Dye, rinse and dry.

More binding may be added and the sample dyed a second colour; or the whole sample can be untied and rearranged so that the blank areas are brought to the fore, and the well textured parts buried in the centre of the tube. Bind as before and dye, in the same or a different colour.

Rinse, dry and untie.

A two-colour effect may be obtained with only one binding, by the following means:

Form the fabric into a tube as described and bind very firmly. Immerse the sample in the dyebath and leave until the dye has penetrated well into the bundle. Squeeze and rinse, but do not dry or untie. Dye again in a very much stronger or contrasting colour, immersing the sample for a much shorter period.

Rinse after the second dyeing. Dry and untie.

This same scheme will work in reverse, making the first dyeing a very short dip and the second for a much longer period, rinsing or not in between, according to the effect desired.

These experiments give a more watery subtle texture. If this is considered inadequate, a much darker dye can be painted on the outer edges of the tube, or the cloth bunched up and bound again and dyed a third colour.

After a little practice with this kind of texturing it is possible to get a marked difference in effect by varying the tension and thickness of the bindings. Fine thread, coarse string or rope can be tried, all of which can be previously dyed.

(b) Twisting and Coiling

This technique is readily adapted to patterning long lengths of cloth. Where two, three or four yards of material are involved, it is advisable to enlist the help of another person, to hold the second end of cloth and to twist it in the opposite direction (326). When it begins to curl back on itself, fold it over in half. As it is more difficult to bind the central portion of a long coil of cloth, the sample may be folded into three, four or more " U " bends (327). This makes it easier to handle, and incidentally cuts down the binding necessary. Tie and secure the two open ends (327X), then bind, to give the type of texture required. Binding may be open, criss-cross ; loosely or closely packed ; in lines or bands ; using thread or thick string (328). Dye, rinse and dry. Untie when dyeing is complete.

For a more evenly distributed pattern, fold the cloth in half or into four lengthwise before twisting and coiling (329). After dyeing and untying, repeat the whole process, refolding the cloth so that the area from the inside comes to the outside and vice versa (330). Dye in one or more colours, rinse and dry. Untie.

A length of cloth may be gathered up and tied at intervals of 12 to 18 inches. These " links " can then be folded and collected together in a bundle. Tie the two open ends (331). Secure one end of the bundle (332). Twist each loop into a circular coil (333), then bind the whole bundle (334).

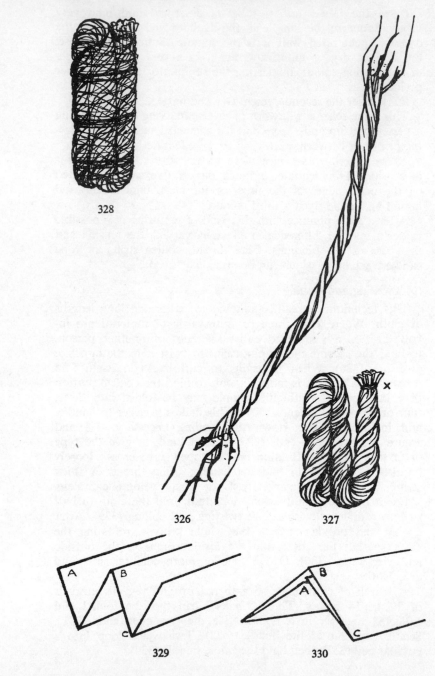

328

326   327

329   330

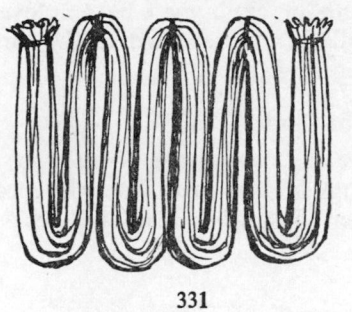

331

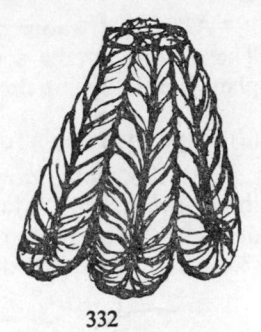

332

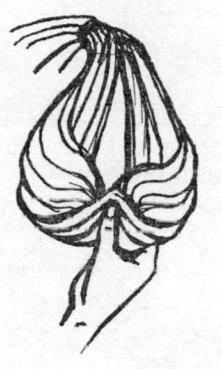

333

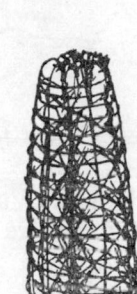

334

If this is bulky leave it longer in the dyebath. Before dyeing a second or third colour untie the binding but leave the bundle tied at one end (332). Untwist the loops, then retwist them in the opposite direction, turning the outer edges to the inside and bringing the inner undyed areas to the outside. Bind, and dye a different colour. Rinse, dry and untie.

A length of cloth may be twisted into a coil, wrapped round a base and bound before dyeing as in 241.

(c) Knotting a Long Length of Cloth

This is carried out in the same way as the smaller sample, but the cloth may be folded in half lengthwise, before being knotted. Repeat the process several times, bringing the parts from the inside of the bundle to the outside in turn. The knots need not necessarily be tied in the same place on the cloth for the second or third dyeing. After each dyeing, rinse, dry, and untie the knots. Repeat until a satisfactory all-over texture is formed.

" All-over " knots on a length of cloth may be employed. These need not be spaced regularly nor repeated in the same place before dyeing the second or third time.

(d) Rope Tying on a full Width of Cloth

Fold the cloth, down or across, into pleats about two or three inches wide. Make bindings at intervals. This will mean drawing the pleats into a smaller compass or making " necks " (335). Dye, rinse and dry.

335

1. Add open binding along the whole sample and dye again.
2. Fold into " U " bends, add binding and dye again.
3. Twist each unbound portion over diagonally (336), add binding and dye (337).

336

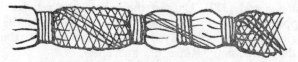

337

4. Dye the edges of the folds a different colour. All the rope and folding techniques can be carried out on a larger scale, using the full width of the material. When a large piece of cloth is being used, to save time, it is possible to fold it in half, across or down, then proceed to mark out and pleat the folds as if working on single cloth. Bind and dye as before.

(e) The Edge or Individual Stripe

This is a most useful method for obtaining a variety of background stripes. Fold and dye several stripes together as one. Other stripes can be dyed at right angles to the first layer.

(f) Clump Tying

Tie medium to large objects in the cloth, at random, or to form a regular repeat. The multi-spot method of picking up points of cloth on a needle, bunching them together and binding as a clump, carried out on a large scale, is an ideal way of arriving at an exciting background texture. Objects may be tied in the cloth some distance apart. Dye, rinse and dry. Collect the clumps together, bind the background and dye in a different colour.

(g) Ruching

Tie the cloth into loops (338) and thread on a piece of wood (339). Bind and dye (340).

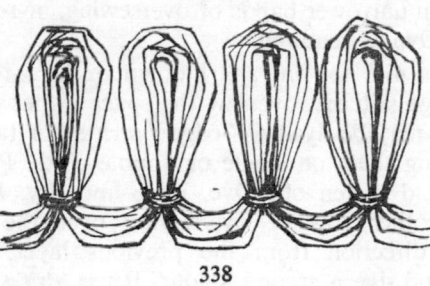

338

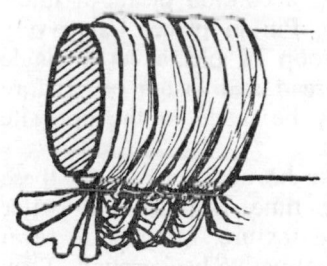

339

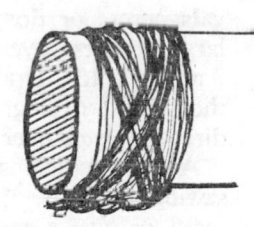

340

(h) Sewing

The following are suggestions for speeding up the sewing process to make good backgrounds.
1. Large stitches and rows farther apart. Binding may be added to help form a resist.

2. Lines of running stitches on double cloth; make wider tucks and fold two or three together to sew as one (189).

3. For an all-over sewn texture, make rows of large tacking stitches 4in. to 8in. apart, pull up tightly and add a little open binding in between the rows.

4. Fold 2in. or 3in. tucks over three times and oversew with large stitches. Tighten threads before dyeing.

5. Using large stitches, tack a " diamond net " (192) arrangement on the cloth. Pull up the threads and add binding, if necessary.

6. Fold the cloth over double widthways. Place pins at intervals from 3in. to 6in. below the fold. Oversew the fold, taking the stitches down to the line of pins. Remove pins. When pulling up this " giant " size oversewing, bunch up the cloth unevenly underneath the stitches. Fasten off. Repeat these tucks over the whole cloth. They can be placed in between narrower bands of oversewing, or rows of tacking stitches. Dye as required.

7. Rule lines 4in. to 8in. apart down or across the material. Using large stitches, oversew the space in between the lines. The lines may be dyed as "edge" stripes, or tacking stitches made along them on single or double cloth. Pull up all the threads and fasten off. Dye, rinse and dry. Do not untie. Make another row of oversewing over the first, in the opposite direction from the previous layer. Pull up the threads and dye a second colour. Rinse, dry and untie.

8. Make sets of three or four large accordion pleats at intervals across or down the fabric. Pin in place. Using very large stitches, oversew each group of pleats, as a single " tuck " (215). Draw up the thread and fasten off. Before the second dyeing, stitches may be made in the opposite direction, back over the first ones.

A little judicious binding may be added to all of these sewing methods, if it will save time, help form a better resist or give a more interesting texture. Large-scale sewn spirals on single cloth make an attractive background. They may also be sewn in the shape of triangles, stars or rectangles.

(i) Binding

The material can be gathered into a tube lengthwise, and covered entirely with open or lattice binding. Add another layer of binding, which may be applied in certain areas, in wide or narrow bands before dyeing a second colour. A much darker dye can be brushed over the outer folds. Rinse, dry and untie. Repeat if necessary.

It is possible to make the material into a tube widthways for the second tying up. Bind and dye. Rinse, dry and untie. Large pieces are best tied in two stages. Fold the cloth in half. Dye the sample with one half to the outside, then untie and repeat the process, bringing the second half to the fore. This will ensure that the texture is more regularly distributed.

Vary the materials for binding—yarn, string, raffia, tape, as well as the usual thread. Dyed threads used at intervals or over the whole sample help to give an interesting quality.

AREAS OF COLOUR

Draw the outlines of any shapes required and sew round them with large tacking stitches. Pull up the threads and fasten off. Add binding where necessary, usually along the drawn up line of sewing. Dye each shape, and rinse individually. When resist shapes are needed on a dyed ground, cover each shape with close binding after drawing up the sewing thread. Immerse the whole sample in the dye. Rinse, dry and untie. A symmetrical shape may be halved, drawn and sewn on double cloth (193-5).

Use the folded stripe method for bands of colour either across or down the sample. Dip the edges of the folds in dye or bind, where required, and dye the whole sample. Add more binding and dye the second colour. Rinse, dry and untie.

For circles pick up a point of cloth and bind, according to the size desired.

The pleated oval or diamond method on a large scale is very useful for backgrounds. Use as a dyed shape, or a resist shape on a dyed ground.

XIII

SEVERAL TECHNIQUES IN ONE DESIGN

AFTER gaining a working knowledge of the craft of tie-and-dye, it should be possible to design patterns of greater interest where several techniques are incorporated.

For instance.

1. A sample which has already been dyed, may have a darker texture superimposed over the whole cloth or in certain parts by the marbling technique. This can be slight or heavy according to the amount of binding added.
2. By adding binding in certain areas the top of a sample may be dyed differently from the bottom, one side a different colour from the other side, or bands of colour added.
3. The folded edges of a "rope" sample may be oversewn before dyeing the second colour.
4. The cloth can be covered with partially drawn-up running or oversewing stitches to give a crinkly appearance. Small objects may then be bound into the cloth at intervals.
5. On fine cloth, outline large circles, squares or diamonds with several rows of running stitches. Draw up the threads and fasten off. Tie the cloth in the centre of each shape into a knot. Dye, rinse and dry. Re-tie the knot and dye a second colour, or dip just the knots in dye. Binding may be added and a third colour dyed.
6. Large bound or sewn stripes may alternate with a line of large clump ties or groups of small clumps.
7. Arrange pleated ovals in rows or place inside sewn ovals or diamonds.
8. Sewn diamonds or ovals can be placed inside large bound shapes.
9. Large oversewn shapes may enclose smaller sewn and bound shapes or clump ties.
10. Oversewing may be combined in many ways, with diamond or oval ruching, added to the string-cases, following the outlines or placed at intervals, as definite shapes.

11. Areas of sewn texture may be combined with bound shapes, knotting or clump tying.
12. Narrow edge stripes can be used to make panels or a diamond net on the cloth. These can be filled in with smaller bound or sewn shapes.

If the pattern is arranged in bands across or down the material, there are infinite ways of ringing the changes. Any two or three of the following would combine to give an interesting design.

13. Single wide edge stripes, or a group of narrow ones.
14. Row of large clump ties, a double row of smaller ones.
15. A single line of stitching on single or double cloth repeated at intervals.
16. A band of oversewing, or several, wide or narrow.
17. A band of stitching to form a texture.
18. A zig-zag band of sewing.
19. A band of ruching, straight, diamond or oval, narrow or wide.
20. A row of ovals, diamonds, or squares sewn on double cloth and bound.
21. A row of bandhana spots, or groups of such rows.
22. A line of medium bound circles.
23. A band of texture made by knotting the fabric.
24. Lines and bands made by the binding method.
25. A row of sewn spirals, round, triangular or square.
26. A row of flower or leaf shapes sewn on double cloth or oversewn, etc.

Multicolour Designs

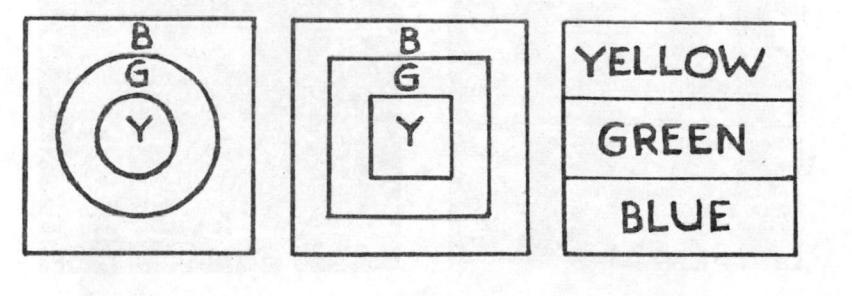

343   344   345

A very simple tie-dye pattern becomes exciting when dyed several colours (343, 344, 345). The sample is bound and dyed

No. 4 or 11. No. 26, then No. 1

No. 10, 11, 18 or 19

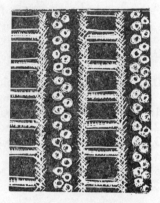

No. 6. No. 10, 15 or 16 and 14

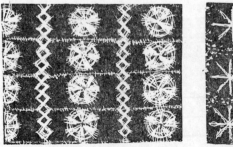

Nos. 15, 20 and 22

Nos. 10 and 1. Nos. 10 and 11, 17 and 26

(Numbers refer to list on pp. 158 and 159)

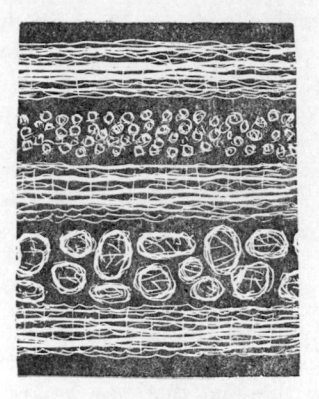

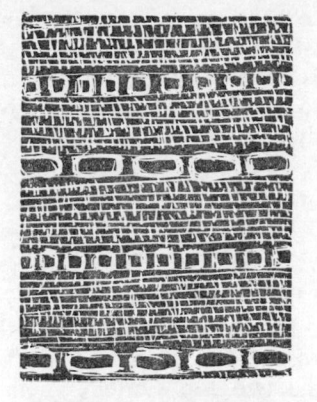

No. 6 or 11. No. 14 or 21 with
15 or 17

No. 6 or 11. No. 4. No. 15,
17 or 24 with 20

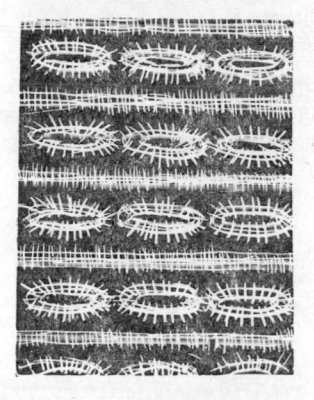

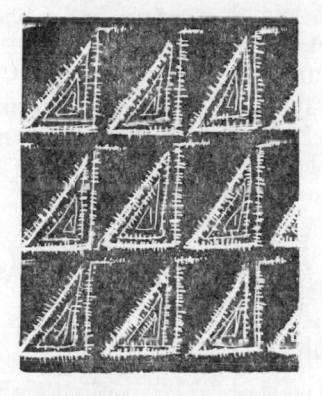

No. 13, 16, 19 or 24 with No.
7, 8 or 20

No. 25 or 10

No. 5, 8, 9 or 20 and 12

(Numbers refer to the list on pp. 158 and 159)

so that areas of each colour are retained besides those made where two or three colours overlap. A concentrated dye liquor is needed. Where fastness to light is unimportant, it is possible to use Basic dyes which give rich, vivid colours, even with dip dyeing.

Method

Tie up cloth for a circle, square or stripe, etc.

Two Colours

Divide the sample into three sections, A, B, and C, lengthwise (346). Make a solid binding just below B (346a). Invert the two top sections A and B into the first dye, say yellow, leaving C undyed and dry. Rinse A and B carefully and squeeze out excess moisture with newspaper or soft rag. Untie binding below B, or leave just a line binding. Make a solid binding at A immediately above B (346b). This can be done before or after the sample is dried. Dip B and C into the second dye, say blue. Rinse, dry and untie. There should now be an area of yellow at A, blue at C, and B, which has received both dyes, should be green. Similarly blue and red will give purple, red and yellow will give orange.

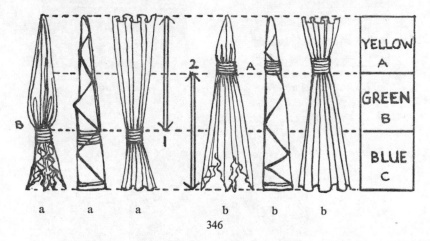

346

Three Colours

Divide sample into six sections, lengthwise, A, B. C, D, E, F. Make a solid binding on D just below C (347a). Invert the top three sections into the first dye, yellow, leaving the three lower sections undyed. Rinse carefully and squeeze. Untie binding at D. Completely cover A and B with solid binding. Make a binding on F just below E (347b). Invert the top of the sample into the second colour, blue, as far as the binding at F, leaving the last section undyed. Rinse thoroughly and squeeze.

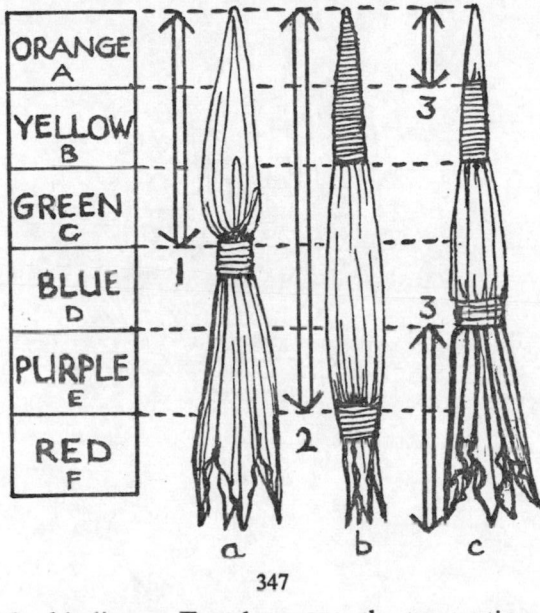

347

Untie the binding at F and uncover the top section, A, leaving B bound solidly. Place binding on D immediately above E (347c).

Invert top section A in the third colour, red. Rinse and squeeze. Dip the two lowest sections F and E in red dye. Rinse, squeeze, dry and untie.

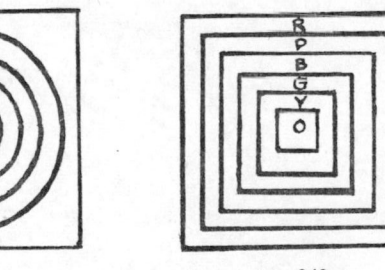

348   349

There should now be areas of orange, yellow, green, blue, purple and red, in that order (348, 349).

An infinite number of colour schemes arranged in any order, bright or more subtle, can be arranged.

Some multicolour effects, for instance large or small circles, ovals, clumps, edge stripes, etc., where each is dyed separately, could be repeated over a large area of cloth (350).

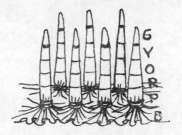

350

XIV

THE DYEING PROCESS

THE choice of dyes for tie-and-dye is governed by many factors ; the kind of equipment available, whether an individual or a group is participating, whether fastness to light is essential and, lastly, the kind of fabric to be dyed.

A stainless steel bowl or saucepan is the ideal dyebath, but enamel, glass and galvanised ware are also suitable. For storing any left over dyes, screw-top jars and bottles are invaluable. It is advisable to mark the date of mixing, the colour and the class of dye, on each jar.

Some form of weighing and measuring of materials, crude though it may be, is necessary, in order to build up a working knowledge of the behaviour and possibilities of each dyestuff. Household balance scales may be used. Where there are no small weights, coins can be substituted.

The following weights may be helpful :

oz	Approx. grams	Coins
$\frac{1}{10}$	$2\frac{3}{4}$	1 sixpenny piece
$\frac{1}{6}$	$5\frac{1}{2}$	1 halfpenny or 1 shilling
$\frac{1}{4}$	$6\frac{3}{4}$	1 threepenny piece (nickel)
$\frac{1}{3}$	$9\frac{1}{2}$	1 penny
$\frac{1}{2}$	13	1 halfcrown or 2 threepenny pieces
$\frac{3}{4}$	$20\frac{1}{4}$	3 threepenny pieces or 1 halfcrown and 1 threepenny piece
1	$28\frac{1}{2}$	3 pennies or 5 halfpennies

I pint weighs $1\frac{1}{4}$ lb or 20 oz: I litre (approx. $1\frac{3}{4}$ pints)= 1000 c.cm.

Allow 1 tablespoonful of water for 1 oz, and 20 tablespoonsful to 1 pint.

As tie-and-dye is a resist dyeing process, the usual rules for producing well-dyed fabrics do not always apply. For this craft the best dye is one that gives a powerful colour in a short time, and does not penetrate the cloth too readily. The dye liquor must be strong enough to give the darkest colour in the design, as the paler colours are produced automatically in the folds of the fabric where the dye only partially penetrates.

The sample is very much reduced in size, owing to the bunching and binding, and therefore needs correspondingly less dye in proportion to its weight. When more than one dyeing is contemplated it is usual to begin with the palest colour and to dye the darkest colour last. However, this is not a hard and fast rule.

Quantity of dye required

For the purposes of tie-and-dye, a wide shallow dye vessel is usually uneconomical. Choose one that just accommodates the sample widthways so that to cover it in depth the minimum amount of dye can be used.

To calculate the quantity of dye liquor needed to dye a sample, this simple expedient may be followed.

Into the dye vessel measure (counting in pints) just enough water to cover the sample. When the number of pints required has been ascertained, estimate the weight of dye powder and other items from the recipes given, multiplying or dividing the quantities in their correct proportions.

Strength of dyes

The recipes given are for single strength dyestuffs, often marked with the letter " S " on the jar or tin. Sometimes the dye powder is stronger. This will be stated on the label. For instance if 150 is placed after the name of the colour it is 50 per cent stronger. If 200, it is twice as strong. Use correspondingly less dye powder for these brands.

A very comprehensive range of colours can be mixed if the following four only are purchased: yellow, blue, red and black.

Cloth should never be dyed unless it has been previously *washed* in soapy water and rinsed. Use a mild soap powder, detergent or Lissapol D ($\frac{1}{2}$ teaspoonful per 2 pints) for this.

It is not absolutely necessary to " wet out " a sample, as in ordinary dyeing, before placing it in the dyebath. It can be entered " wet " or dry. A wetted sample gives a sharper resist. Another variation is to enter the sample into the first colour dry, rinse, then place it in the second colour whilst wet and without adding to the bindings.

Colour test

Make a colour test on a piece of cloth similar to that of the sample before commencing to dye. Note the length of time that the test sample is immersed in the dye, so that if the colour is too pale or too dark the dyeing time can be adjusted.

Water

Soft water is best for dyeing. Rain-water if unpolluted by the atmosphere is ideal. Where the water is very hard " Calgon " water softener may be used. The quantities necessary are given on the tin. Approximately $\frac{1}{4}$ teaspoonful to 1 pint is sufficient.

Exhaustion

A dye is said to be " exhausted " when all the colouring matter has been transferred to the fabric. This usually takes longer to effect than the time that a tie-and-dye sample can be left in the dyebath. Which means there is still colouring matter left in the dye liquor. It may be possible to use this for paler colours or for shading another coloured dye. The deeper shades of most dyes are faster to light than paler tones of the same colour.

Rinsing

After every dyeing operation a sample must be rinsed thoroughly until the water is clear.

If a sample is dyed three colours it is necessary to rinse after each dyeing.

When certain parts only have been dyed, rinse these separately, then rinse the whole sample. With packet and direct dyes a preliminary rinse can be made in a small amount of water. This will contain enough dyestuff to use for mixing in with another or a paler colour.

When the dyeing processes have been completed, the sample dried and untied, rinse once more, to remove any loose dye that may be lingering in the folds of cloth.

BLEACHING

Some dyes can be bleached out partially or completely by household bleach or Dygon (except Caledon and Reactive dyes).

This means that the tie-and-dye process may be carried out in reverse, by tying up a previously dyed length of cloth and immersing it in bleach. In this case the bindings reserve the pattern in colour, whilst the background is bleached.

As bleaches vary in strength, it is difficult to stipulate the correct proportion of bleach to water necessary to remove any particular dye. Make a test on a small piece of the dyed cloth to find out whether the dye is dischargeable and the correct proportion of bleach to water required for the purpose.

Begin with a weak solution (1 part bleach to 6 parts water, or ½ teaspoonful Dygon to 1 pint boiling water) and add to it rather than have one so strong that it rots the fabric.

The sample may be designed to consist of :

(a) A completely bleached pattern.

(b) Certain parts of the design bleached.

(c) A slight discharge incorporated in the main pattern.

(a) A completely bleached pattern

Dye a length of cloth with a dischargeable dye.

Tie up the material according to the pattern planned. Prepare and test the bleach solution. Immerse the sample in the solution until the surface colour has been discharged. Rinse very thoroughly at once. Dry and untie. Rinse again.

(b) Certain areas bleached

Leave some plain areas on a tied-up sample. Dye with a dischargeable dye.

1. Then tie up the areas to be bleached and dip each one separately into the bleach solution. Rinse separately. Untie and rinse the whole sample thoroughly.

2. Or tie up the areas to be bleached. Bind the rest of the sample very firmly. Immerse the sample in the bleach solution. Rinse and untie, then rinse the whole sample again.

3. Or tie up the areas to be bleached. With a piece of cotton wool dab the bleach on them until the colour is discharged. The bleach may need to be a little stronger for this. A small piece of cloth or cotton wool tied round the end of a pencil, wooden skewer or paint brush handle is convenient for applying bleach. Rinse, untie and rinse again.

(c) A slight discharge

A tie-and-dye cloth previously dyed, where perhaps the resist is not too pronounced, can be bleached in parts to emphasise the existing pattern.

Leave the areas to be bleached unbound and protruding. Cover the parts that are to be safeguarded from the bleach. Apply bleach to the required areas until the colour is discharged. Rinse, untie, then rinse the whole sample again.

If a design of fine lines and small dots is desired, use a pad impregnated with bleach. To make this, place two or three layers of cloth soaked in bleach on a saucer, lid or shallow bowl. Allow the tips of the spots or edges of the folded cloth to just touch the pad. Repeat until the desired amount of bleaching has been achieved. Rinse, untie and rinse the whole sample again.

DYES FOR TIE-AND-DYE

The dyeing instructions given must be repeated for each colour used. This applies to all dyes.

With dyes which are likely to be used in schools the quantities have been simplified and are given in "spoonfuls". These represent level spoonfuls measured in the standard plastic spoon "scoops" obtainable from hardware shops in groups of 4 sizes, $\frac{1}{4}$, $\frac{1}{2}$, 1 teaspoon and 1 tablespoon.

The amounts allowed for in the following recipes are:

    1 teaspoon dye powder   = approx. 5 grammes
    1 tablespoon common salt = approx. 15 grammes
    1 tablespoon common soda = approx. 20 grammes
    1 tablespoon Glauber's salt = approx. 20 grammes

The quantities given refer to common washing soda, Glauber salt crystals and to common salt. If soda ash, calcined or anhydrous chemicals are used, halve the quantities given in the recipes.

Urea helps to dissolve the dye powder when a strong dye liquor is being prepared. Its use is not essential for tie-and-dye, except that it might help to dissolve reactive dyes when using the cold dyeing method. Dissolve 2 teaspoons urea in $\frac{1}{2}$ pint boiling water, stir. Use this solution warm, to mix dye powder.

Household Dyes

Dylon Multipurpose, Dylon Liquid, Drummer, Rit, Tintex dyes or similar will dye most fabrics and some have fairly good light fastness. Wash tie-dyed fabrics in warm water (plus a little mild soap powder or detergent) to minimise staining of the resists. Rinse well and dry quickly. Cover with newspaper when ironing.

Hot Dyeing

Method

Paste the dye from 1 container (or 2 teaspoons) with cold water. Add 2–3 pints hot water. Add salt or vinegar as directed. Stir.

Liquid dyes: Add 1 cap measure to 2–3 pints of hot water and stir. Wet out sample if required and dye just below the boil for 1–20 minutes. The longer time in the dye produces a deeper colour. Rinse. Dry. Add more binding before dyeing the next colour. Repeat the dyeing process. Rinse. Dry. Untie. Rinse again. Roll the sample in newspaper or cloth to extract excess liquid after rinsing; this speeds up the drying. Dry quickly and iron while damp, covering the sample with newspaper to prevent the colour from spreading. Large articles can be put in a spin-dryer.

A sample which has been completely immersed in the dye for one or more colours can then have certain parts, one end or any projecting tips dyed a different colour. Enclose the parts of the sample not to be dyed in a polythene bag and to prevent the dye from seeping up, bind firmly around the opening. This leaves the tips free to be inverted into shallow dye liquor. Dye may also be applied to specific areas with a brush or with a piece of cotton wool tied to the end of a pencil. Rinse as directed above.

Cold Dyeing with Household Dyes

Some teachers find that cold dyeing can be undertaken by the youngest schoolchildren. The same depth of colour is not obtained with cold dyeing as with hot dyeing, but attractive pastel colours are produced.

Method

The dye will probably have to be mixed beforehand, but if it can be mixed in the classroom so that the dye is still warm the colours will be deeper.

Paste the dye from one container (or 2 teaspoons) with water. Add 1½–2 pints boiling water and salt or vinegar as directed. Stir.

Liquid dyes: Add 1 cup measure to 1–1½ pints boiling water. Stir.

Bring the dye liquor to the boil in both cases, if possible after mixing. Dye as directed for hot dyes. Different coloured dyes can be mixed together dry or in liquid form.

Basic Dyes

These dyes give rich brilliant colours even with a short dip in cold dye liquor, but unfortunately they fade badly.

They are suitable for cotton, linen, viscose rayon, silk, wool and some mixture fabrics.

Cotton and Viscose Rayon

The cloth must be mordanted and fixed, before being dyed, as follows :

Mordant

Mix 2 oz tannic acid with 5 pints cold water, until dissolved.

Soak the material in this bath for 24 hours, or enter the cloth, heat to 140 deg. F. (60 deg. C.) gradually, and leave to cool for 2 hours.

Squeeze the surplus liquid from the cloth and dry without rinsing.

Fixing

Work the sample for 3 minutes in a bath containing 1 oz tartar emetic (antimony potassium tartrate) dissolved in 5 pints of cold water, and add $\frac{1}{2}$ oz. of chalk (calcium carbonate).

Rinse in cold water and dry.

Dyeing

For a strong colour, paste $\frac{1}{4}$ oz dye powder with a small quantity of acetic acid (30 per cent).

Add 2 to 4 pints cold soft water and stir.

Heat gradually but do not boil.

Test for colour. Wet out the sample if necessary.

Dip the sample in the dye for a few seconds.

Squeeze out surplus dye, rinse very thoroughly and dry.

Basic dye may be brushed or dabbed on to the sample.

Rinse after each dyeing operation.

Wool and Silk

Basic dyes may be used for wool and silk. These need not be mordanted. Allow a longer dyeing time than for cotton. Add a little acetic acid to the dye liquor.

When the water is hard, add extra acetic acid to the dyebath.

The dyes may be mixed together in the liquid or powder form.

Although basic and direct dyes may not be mixed together, dyed with direct dye. The sample, in this case, does not require it is possible to dye a sample with basic dye after it has been mordanting, as the direct dye acts as a mordant for the basic dye.

Articles and garments to be used in artificial light may be satisfactorily dyed with basic dyes. Their extreme richness of colour makes them particularly attractive for the stage. Designers too will find them invaluable.

Basic dyes are exceptionally good for discharging, with Dygon or household bleach. The reaction is very quick so that the sample should be taken from the bleach after a few seconds and then rinsed thoroughly--see pp. 167–169.

Direct Dyes

These are good "all round" dyes, some having very good light fastness and are suitable for cotton, linen, viscose rayon; some selected dyes are suitable for silk and wool. A warm wash only is recommended for the dyed fabrics, otherwise the resists become stained. (See remarks about Household dyes.)

Hot Dyeing Method
Recipe 1 simplified

Paste ½ teaspoon dye powder with a little cold water. Add 1 pint hot water and 2 *tablespoons* salt. Stir.

Recipe 2

Paste ½ oz or 14 grammes dye powder with a little water. Add 4–6 pints or 2–4 litres hot water according to depth of colour required.

Add 3¼ oz or 90 grammes salt. Stir.

Heat gradually until almost boiling. Wet out the sample if required and dye at this temperature for 10 minutes—1 hour, stirring occasionally. A longer dyeing time gives a deeper colour. Rinse well until water clears. Dry.

Add more binding before dyeing further colours. When the final dyeing is completed, rinse thoroughly. Dry. Untie. Rinse again and dry quickly. Iron while damp covered with newspaper. The only objection to untying while the sample is wet is the danger of staining the resists. To minimise this, plunge the sample in cold water immediately it is untied, then roll or pat it between sheets of newspaper, dry quickly and iron while still damp covered with newspaper.

Recipe 3

Cold Dyeing for medium shades only.

Paste 1 teaspoon dye powder with a little water, add 1 pint hot water and 2–3 tablespoons salt. Bring to the boil. Follow instructions for hot dyeing.

Direct dyes can be superimposed over most dyes as a final layer of colour. Direct dyes can be mixed together. A large sample with densely packed folds will need to be dyed longer even than 1 hour. Put it in the dyebath dry, and add the salt at 15-minute intervals. If the dye becomes exhausted add some freshly mixed colour to it. After dyeing, leave the sample in the dyebath until it cools.

Acid Dyes

These are excellent for silk and wool. The colours are bright and intense. Some have very good light fastness. It is advisable to wash in warm water only, rinse in warm water and dry quickly.

Recipe 1 simplified

Paste ½ teaspoon dye with water. Add 1 pint hot water.
Add 2 tablespoons Glauber's salt and 1 teaspoon acetic acid 30 per cent. Stir.

Recipe 2

Paste ½ oz or 14 grammes dye powder with a little water.
Add 1¼ oz or 50 grammes Glauber's salt.
Add 3–6 pints or 2–4 litres hot water.
Add 1 oz or 28 cc or 1 tablespoon acetic acid 30%. Stir.
Wet out sample if required, place in the hot dye and dye at this temperature (85°C 95°C) (190°F–200°F) for 5 minutes to 30 minutes (longer if necessary). Rinse in warm water. Dry.
Add more binding before dyeing further colours. Finally rinse and dry. Untie and rinse again preferable in warm water. Iron while damp covered with newspaper. These dyes can be mixed together.

Caledon Vat Dyes

These are very fast to light and washing, suitable for dyeing cotton, linen and viscose rayon and can be used for silk.

The following colours form a comprehensive range which (apart from black) can be dyed at 120 deg. F (50 deg. C), or, after being vatted, those marked * will dye cold.

* Caledon Yellow 5 GK	* Caledon Olive R	
* ,, Gold Orange 3 G	* ,, Brown R	
* ,, Brilliant Orange 6 R	,, Dark Brown 3 R	
* ,, Brilliant Violet R	,, Brilliant Red 3 B	
* ,, Brilliant Blue 3 G	,, Green 7 G	
* ,, Jade Green XN	,, Direct Black AC	

Use Olive instead of Black for shading. Other colours can be mixed together, preferably after being vatted separately, although it is possible to mix them in powder form.

Always use a thermometer to maintain the correct temperature. If the dye solution becomes too hot the vat will be ruined. Use rubber gloves when handling the dyed sample.

Turning the dye stuff which is insoluble in water into a soluble compound is known as " vatting." There are two stages in the dyeing process :

Method

To make approximately three pints of dye liquor.

Vat $\begin{cases} \frac{1}{4} \text{ oz dye powder single strength and } \frac{1}{2} \text{ pint soft water} \\ \frac{1}{8} \text{ oz caustic soda flakes, or 10 c.cm. caustic soda solution} \\ \quad \text{(78 deg. Tw, 38 deg. Be),} \\ \frac{1}{8} \text{ oz sodium hydrosulphite.} \end{cases}$

Dyebath $\begin{cases} 2\frac{1}{2} \text{ pints soft water and 2-3 oz common salt} \\ \frac{1}{8} \text{ oz caustic soda flakes or 10 c.cm. caustic soda} \\ \quad \text{solution (78 deg. Tw, 38 deg. Be),} \\ \frac{1}{8} \text{ oz sodium hydrosulphite.} \end{cases}$

Stage 1, preparing the vat

In an enamel basin or jam jar, paste the dye powder with a little methylated spirits or Turkey Red Oil. Add 8 tablespoonsful of soft water and stir thoroughly. Place the basin in a saucepan containing water and heat to 120 deg. F. (50 deg. C.).

Put 4 tablespoonsful of cold water in a jam jar, then add $\frac{1}{4}$ oz caustic soda flakes and stir until dissolved. Put *half* this caustic soda solution into the vat (with the dye powder) and stir.

Next add $\frac{1}{8}$ oz hydrosulphite, stirring very gently so that no air bubbles are formed. Maintain at 120 dec. F., (50 deg. C.) for 10 minutes, stirring gently occasionally.

Stage 2, preparing the dyebath

While the dye is vatting put $2\frac{1}{2}$ pints of soft water into the dyebath. Add most of the remaining caustic soda solution and stir. Add $\frac{1}{8}$ oz hydrosulphite and stir gently, raising the temperature to 120 deg. F. (50 deg. C.).

When the vat is ready it will have changed colour and be free from specks. Empty the basin containing the vat gently into the dyebath, bring the temperature up to 120 deg. F., 50 deg. C. Add salt and stir. Dye the sample from 1-10 minutes at 120 deg. F. (50 deg. C.). It is possible to dye in a cold or luke-warm liquor, but most colours have the maximum affinity for the cloth when dyed at 120 deg. F. (50 deg. C.).

If the dyebath shows any signs of changing back to its original colour, or specks are apparent, add a little hydrosulphite and the remains of the caustic soda solution, leave for a few minutes, then stir and resume dyeing. Test papers can be obtained for checking that the correct quantities of these chemicals are present in the dyebath.

A *Caledon Yellow G.N.* paper is turned blue if there is an excess of hydrosulphite present in the bath.

A *Phenolphthalein* paper will turn magenta when a drop of dye is put on it if there is an excess of caustic soda.

When the dyeing is completed remove the sample from the dyebath and squeeze. Do not rinse. Hang the sample up to oxidise for twenty minutes in an airy spot away from the sun-light. For a stronger colour re-dip for 1 to 2 minutes, once or twice, adding a little salt and caustic soda to the dyebath. Squeeze and oxidise after each dip.

Rinse very thoroughly in cold water and then soak for 5 minutes in five pints of water to which has been added a few spots of sulphuric acid 10 per cent or one tablespoonful of acetic acid 30 per cent. Rinse well. Dry and *untie*. Boil the sample for 5 minutes in soft water and soapflakes (2 table-spoonsful to 4 pints of water).

Rinse and iron while damp. Repeat the process for each colour. Black must be vatted and dyed at 140 deg. F. (60 deg. C.), needs a little less hydrosulphite and salt but more caustic soda.

Caledon Vat Dyes for Silk

Prepare the vat as for cotton but with less caustic soda ($\frac{1}{8}$ oz instead of $\frac{1}{4}$ oz in 2 tablespoonsful of water).

Use most of this for the vat. *Do not* put any in the dyebath, use more salt instead.

Dye for 1 to 5 minutes. Oxidise in a draught for 10 to 15 minutes. Soak in the acid for 10 minutes. Rinse and untie. Wash in hot soapy water (but do *not* boil) for 5 to 10 minutes. Rinse and iron while damp.

Sodium Hydrosulphite ($Na_2S_2O_4$) soon deteriorates; buy in small quantities, do not expose to the air any more than is essential. Seal the opening of the container with Sellotape immediately after using and wrap in a polythene bag.

Caustic soda (sodium hydroxide) should also be kept air-tight.

Indigo may be vatted in the same way as the Caledons and used lukewarm for dip dyeing (three to four times) for periods of 8, 6, 4 and 2 minutes, oxidising the sample in between each dip.

Dispersed Dyestuffs

These will dye polyester, nylon and acetate rayon.

Method

Paste ¼ oz dye powder with warm water, add 4–6 pints water and heat to 190°F (85°C). Dye at this temperature for 1–30 minutes. Squeeze out surplus dye; rinse. Dry. Add binding before dyeing further colours. Finally rinse, dry, untie, rinse again and iron while damp.

Reactive Dyes

These fast-to-light dyes give bright colours on cotton (especially mercerised), linen, viscose rayon, and to a lesser degree on silks and woollens. They are fixed on the fibre by direct chemical linkage, the dye molecule becoming part of the cellulosic molecule, so they are very fast to washing.

These dyes penetrate rather readily so are useful for dyeing bulky or closely bound samples, particularly those of the folding techniques. Always wet out smaller finely tied bundles or the resist will be lost. Sometimes after untying there seems to be no resist pattern left, but after rinsing and soaping at the boil, the loose dyestuff is washed away and the resists will appear. The two reactive dyestuffs dealt with here are Procion M (*not* the *H* brands) and Dylon Cold Water dyes. Dylon Cold Water dyes are based on the I.C.I. Procion M dyes, so to save confusion the instructions given apply to both. Procion M dyes are more concentrated so less dye powder is needed in the recipes. The two kinds of dyes can be used together on the same sample and can even be mixed together. This gives an attractive and wide colour range.

For these dyes, it is most important that the fabric should be well washed and absorbent, otherwise the dye will not react properly with the fibres and the colour will be washed away during rinsing. Wash the fabric for ½ hour in very hot water with ½ teaspoon Lissapol D per 2 pints water (2 grammes per litre) or soap powder or detergent added. Rinse thoroughly.

For tie dyeing cottons, linens and viscose rayon the following dyeing methods are recommended:

Standard Recipe

1 tin Dylon cold water dye (10 grammes or 2 teaspoon)
  or 1 teaspoon Procion M dye.
4 tablespoons salt.
1 tablespoon soda.
2 pints water.

Dissolve dye powder in 1 pint warm water and stir. In a separate container dissolve the salt and soda in 1 pint hot water and stir.

When the sample is ready and has been wetted out and *not* before then, mix the two solutions together and stir. Place the sample in the dye liquor immediately and move about constantly for the first 10 minutes and at intervals during the rest of the dyeing time. This is very important as the dye tends to react with the water rather than the fabric if it is not moved about.

1. Long cold dyeing method: follow standard recipe and dye cold or at room temperature for 1 hour.
2. Shorter cold dyeing method. Follow standard recipe and dye for 20 minutes–½ hour. This does not give quite such a powerful colour.
3. Short cold dyeing + polythene bag. Follow standard recipe and dye for 20 minutes. Lift the sample out of the dyebath and, without rinsing, put it into a polythene bag. Tie up the ends. Leave 12–24 hours in room temperature or 1–2 hours near (but not touching) a radiator or some similar place where it is warm but not too hot.
4. Short cold dyeing + steaming. Follow standard recipe and dye for 20 minutes. Steam for 5–10 minutes. If no steamer is available, wrap the sample in newspaper (without rinsing it) and if it is not too large place it in a bowl inside a saucepan and steam with the lid on. A kitchen steamer can be used or a gas boiler if the sample is well wrapped in newspaper.
5. Short cold dyeing + baking. Follow standard recipe and dye for 20 minutes. Without rinsing, wrap the sample in newspaper or cloth and place in an ordinary electric oven. Bake for 5 minutes at 140°C (285°F).

Hot Dyeing

All the above methods can be carried out with the dye at a

higher temperature. This may give better colour yields with some of the dyes. Dye at room temperature or up to 70°C (160°F) but no higher than this.

After the dyeing has been completed for *all* methods proceed as follows: Rinse thoroughly until water clears. This may take several rinses as a great deal of loose dye comes away. Wash for 5 minutes in boiling water to which has been added a little Lissapol D, soap powder or detergent. Move sample about. Rinse, untie and rinse again. The sample can be undone while it is wet. A second hot wash after the sample is untied is beneficial and cleans up the resists considerably. Iron while damp.

Before dyeing a second or subsequent colours rinse the sample thoroughly to remove all unfixed dye (a hot soapy wash ensures good results) then add to or rearrange the bindings, undoing some, to release white cloth for the new colour to dye. Very exciting pattern effects are produced by these dyes if the sample is completely untied, rearranged and re-tied, in between dyeing each colour. In this way the design is distributed more evenly over the cloth, and, as each layer remains intact, gives a rich interchange of colour and shape.

Silk

In place of the salt use 2 tablespoons Glauber's salt and only 1 teaspoon soda. Dye for 1 hour at 50°C (120°F). Rinse and wash off in warm water as described.

Chlorinated Wool

Dissolve 1 teaspoon Procion M or 2 teaspoon Dylon Cold Dye in ¼ pint warm water. To 1¾ pints warm water (if greens and blues are to be dyed) add ¾ teaspoon ammonium acetate. *Or* to 1¾ pints warm water (if yellows, red, oranges, browns are to be dyed) add ½ teaspoon acetic acid 30 per cent. Place the dry tied-up sample in the above solution for 5–10 minutes, then add the pre-dissolved dye solution. Stir. Raise the temperature gradually up to the boil and dye for 1 hour. Rinse and wash in warm water. Untie, rinse again and iron while damp. Repeat the process for subsequent colours. The final rinse can include a small quantity of "Soft Rinse" or "Comfort" or any similar agent for softening wool. Once soda has been added to the dye solution it is only effective as a dye for 2–3 hours. If the dye must be mixed some time before it is needed, put the dye solution and the salt/soda solution in two separate bottles, mixing equal quantities of each as required. Tightly corked like this the dye can be used over several days. If only a part of a tin of dye is used, keep the remainder in an airtight container. When several colours are to be dyed, or if a class of pupils wish to use different coloured dyes, it saves time to mix up a large quantity of salt/soda solution in a bucket. For instance: 1 gallon hot water, 32 tablespoons salt + 8 tablespoons soda.

The dye powder can then be mixed up, as or when it is wanted, in very small or large quantities, using the standard recipe of 1 teaspoon Procion M dye or 2 teaspoons Dylon Cold Dye per 1 pint warm water. Equal quantities of the two solution are then combined when the sample is ready to be dyed.

Procion dyes and Dylon Cold water will react with Brentamine Fast Black K salt to produce rich brown shades.

Brentamine Fast Black K Salt

Method

After the tied up sample has been dyed in Procion M or Dylon Cold water dyes, dry it *without* rinsing. Add more binding to reserve the existing colours, then dip it in the following solution for approximately 5–10 minutes, or until the colour changes.

Disolve 1–2 teaspoons Brentamine Fast Black K salt in 1 pint warm water, add 1½ tablespoons salt, and stir. Rinse, wash in boiling water for 5 minutes with soap or detergent added. Rinse and untie. Rinse again and iron while damp.

Suggested list of Procion M dyes for tie-and-dye:

Procion	Billiant Yellow	M 4G (Lemon)
„	Yellow	M R (bright golden yellow)
„	Brilliant Orange	M 2R (Flame)
„	Red Brown	M 4R (Mahogany)
„	Brilliant Red	M 5B (Crimson)
„	Brilliant Red	M 8B (Magenta)
„	Scarlet	M G
„	Blue	M 3G (green blue)
„	Navy Blue	M 3R
„	Olive Green	M 3G

Suggested colour mixes:

Black—1 part Brilliant Orange M 2R + 5 parts Blue M 3G.
Brown—I part Blue M 3G + 5 parts Brilliant Orange M 2R.
Equal quantities of A 13 and A 17 Dylon cold water dyes gives a dark charcoal.

Potassium Permanganate

These crystals, dissolved, can be used to dye cotton, linen, rayon and are especially good on wool and silk. The crystals are cheap and easy to obtain and although they fade badly they are useful for early tie and dye experiments.

Method

Dissolve $\frac{1}{2}$ teaspoon crystals in $\frac{1}{2}$ pint hot water. Wet out and immerse the tied-up samples for 5 seconds–5 minutes. Take them out of the liquid and leave them to change colour from purple to brown. Several dips built up a deeper colour. Rinse, wash and untie.

Discharge

Dye a piece of cloth as above. Dry. Tie up very firmly. Dip in fresh or P. L. J. lemon juice until the colour begins to bleach. Rinse, untie and rinse again. The lemon juice can be applied to specific areas of the tied-up bundle—or parts of it dipped in the lemon juice.

Iron rust
Method

Dissolve 1 lb ferrous sulphate (copperas) in 1 gallon hot water. Add $\frac{1}{2}$ lb. lead acetate (poison). Allow to stand overnight. Strain off the green liquid and throw away the sediment immediately or it will harden. Immerse the tied-up sample for one hour in the green liquid, drain on newspaper and dry. Caustic soda solution: Dissolve 3 oz. caustic soda in 1 gallon of cold water (put the caustic soda *into* the cold water gradually, stirring meanwhile). Put the sample in the caustic soda solution and leave for 2 minutes. Drain on newspaper and air dry. Rinse thoroughly and wash in hot soapy water.

Indigo
Method

To make approximately 2 pints.

Mix 1 teaspoon Indigo grains 60 per cent with a little warm water. Dissolve $\frac{1}{2}$ teaspoon caustic soda flakes and $\frac{1}{2}$ teaspoon sodium hydrosulphite in a little cold water and add to 2 pints warm water. Gently add $1\frac{1}{2}$ teaspoon salt and the warm Indigo solution, without making any air bubbles. Stir gently with a glass rod after a few minutes. Allow to vat for 10 minutes or until it has become a yellowish green colour.

Maintain the vat at blood heat whilst dyeing. Enter the sample without making too many air bubbles and dye for 10 minutes. Remove, squeeze and allow to oxidise in the air until it changes to blue; this will take 5–10 minutes. To build up a deeper colour dye the sample again for 3 minutes, remove, squeeze and re-oxidise. Repeat this process until the desired colour is obtained.

If the dyebath turns blue it needs sharpening with the addition of a small quantity of caustic soda and sodium hydrosulphite (previously dissolved in a little cold water). The dyed fabric is rinsed in cold water with 1 teaspoon acetic acid (or a little vinegar) added. Untie. Wash in warm soapy water, rinse and iron while damp.

Identification of Fibres

To make tests, a thread of the fabric is placed in contact with a naked flame. Reactions are:

Wool and silk burn slowly, smell of burnt hair or feathers, leave a black bead of ash.

Cotton, Linen, Viscose rayon burn rapidly, smell of burnt paper, leave very little white ash.

Nylon, Terylene do not burn, but shrink from the flame; melt into a hard round ball which cannot be crushed by the fingers. Nylon gives off a smell similar to that of celery. Terylene gives off an aromatic odour. Nylon dissolves in formic acid.

Acetate Rayon burns slowly, without smell, melts into a black bead which shrinks away from the flame. It can be crushed between the fingers. Dissolves in acetone.

* * *

Suppliers

Dylon International Ltd.,
139 Sydenham Road,
London, S.E.26

Supply in various sizes: Procion M dyes. Dylon cold water dyes. Dygon, Dylon multipurpose dyes. Dylon Liquid dyes. Lissapol D, Urea, Brentamine Fast Black K Salt. Price list available.

Skilbeck Bros. Ltd.,
Bagnall House,
55–57 Glengall Road,
London, S.E.15

Supply in 2 lb tins: Most ICI dyes, also their own brands of dyes. Direct dyes—"Solamine" Acid "Fast FB" colours (will also dye nylon). Dispersed "Cetyls", Caledons. Price list available.

Pronk, Davis and Rusby Ltd.,
44 Penton Street,
London, N.1

Supply in 1 oz, 4 oz and 1 lb packets: Direct—"Fibrajax"
Acid—"Lanajax". Basic—"Lacajax". Disperse—"Celajax".
Price list available.

A wide range of dyes are supplied in 3 lb tins by:

Bayers Dyestuff Ltd.,
Kingsway House,
18–24 Paradise Road,
Richmond,
Surrey

Comak Chemicals Ltd.,
Moon Street,
London, N.1

Supply in ½ lb. or 1 lb. packs: indigo powder, hydrosulphite
and other chemicals.

In ¼ lb, ½ lb and 1 lb quantities: All CIBA dyes. The following can be specified: Direct dyes—CIBA Chlorantine. Acid
dyes—CIBA Cibalan. Reactive dyes—CIBA Cibacron.

The above firms are those known to the author, but there are
many other dye firms that may have excellent products.